TENNYSON'S *"MAUD"* AND ITS CRITICAL, CULTURAL, AND LITERARY CONTEXTS

Tennyson's *"Maud"* and Its Critical, Cultural, and Literary Contexts

Priscilla J. Glanville

Mellen Studies in Literature
English and American Studies
Volume 37

The Edwin Mellen Press
Lewiston•Queenston•Lampeter

Library of Congress Cataloging-in-Publication Data

Glanville, Priscilla J.
    Tennyson's "Maud" and its critical, cultural, and literary contexts / Priscilla J. Glanville.
       p. cm. -- (Mellen studies in literature. English and American studies ; v. 37)
    Includes bibliographical references and index.
    ISBN-0-7734-7134-0
    1. Tennyson, Alfred Tennyson, Baron, 1809-1892. Maud. I. Title. II. Series.

PR5567 .G58 2002
821'.8--dc21

2002070999

This is volume 37 in the continuing series
Mellen Studies in Literature/
English and American Studies
Volume 37 ISBN 0-7734-7134-0
MSL/EAS Series ISBN 0-7734-4209-X

A CIP catalog record for this book is available from the British Library.

The Edwin Mellen Press
Box 450
Lewiston, New York
USA 14092-0450

The Edwin Mellen Press
Box 67
Queenston, Ontario
CANADA L0S 1L0

The Edwin Mellen Press, Ltd.
Lampeter, Ceredigion, Wales
UNITED KINGDOM SA48 8LT

Printed in the United States of America

Dedication

For never missing a ceremony in which my work was recognized, for countless Sundays spent in dusty libraries and evenings idled away before microfilm readers, I would like to dedicate this work to my dear husband, David DiLuzio, and my brother, William Glanville. Thank you, William and David. Your love and support lay the foundations upon which my happiest moments and best work are constructed.

Table of Contents

Preface

Priscilla Glanville's study of Tennyson's *Maud* vibrates with its author's sheer enthusiasm and intensity. Dr. Glanville weaves her examination into the major movements of British Victorian literature: pejoratively by contrast with the Spasmodic movement, affirmatively with the Pre-Raphaelite revolution, and triumphantly with Tennyson's own epigrammatic designation of *Maud* as his "little *Hamlet*."

In Chapter One, Glanville laments that Tennyson's favorite dramatic work, written at the zenith of his remarkable poetic career, continues to be "shamefully under-represented" by contemporary critics in the massive codex of his poetic productivity. Although clearly a product of "both the Romantic sensibility and the Victorian social and religious frameworks, it takes its due position in the critical studies of neither." Samuel Chew considered that in writing *Maud* Alfred Lord Tennyson was influenced by the Spasmodic poets [Alexander Smith, Sydney Dobell, Phillip Bailey], and that such is evident in "the discontinuity of the thought and extravagance of the style." However, Glanville proclaims that "when we take a second look at *Maud*, we find a tragedy on a grand scale, washed in the mysticism of Pre-Raphaelitism and executed with painstaking intricacy and detail: a work that far surpasses anything penned by the school of poets known as the Spasmodics."

When I wrote my first study of Tennyson, *The Two Voices* (1964), the critical mood was quite ready to accept the double direction of major Victorian writers. However, when my second study, *Tennyson's Epic Drama* (1997), appeared, there was little critical response to the claim that the great master of lyric melancholy might also be considered a dramatic writer, regardless of the six plays which were written at the height of his powers and which he considered among his best work.

Thus, although James Smetham noted of the Spasmodics: "I can't say I was ever carried off my feet by them," William Aytoun accused the Spasmodics of

i

"exaggerated Byronism," and Jerome Buckley had to admit that they "neglected overall theme and action to magnify isolated emotions . . . often quite irrelevant to the given mood," Buckley and others could still claim Tennyson as an heir and exponent of the Spasmodics. It is essentially against this designation that Dr. Glanville draws her double aim, at the Spasmodics' bombast and in support of Tennyson's study of melancholy and madness. Hers is a trenchant comparison well worth the reading.

Charles Kingsley understood the subtle accuracy of Tennyson's depiction of pathos that led to madness, with the added quip that in the wake of crowded madhouses *Maud* was highly relevant to its own age. However, the *Westminster Review* expressed the dominant critical response: the Victorians could not accept the "morbidity" of the monodrama, even from their leading poet-prophet. It was not until 1944 that Roy Basler was able to point out that "The plot of the poem . . . is not based primarily upon the conventional love theme . . . but rather upon the theme of psychic conflict between the phases of the hero's personality . . . a drama of the soul in which different phases of passion in one person [monodrama] take the place of different characters."

Dr. Glanville's chapter (Two) on the relation of *Maud* to the Pre-Raphaelite painters is as affirmative as the consideration of the Spasmodics is pejorative. Reminding us that in Moxon's 1837 volume of Tennyson's poems, out of fifty-four illustrations, twenty-nine were by the well-known PRB artists Millais, Hunt, and Rossetti, she then links their shared focus on tiny objects to Darwin's scientific multiplicity, to phantasmagoric hallucinations, and to madness. Echoing the oft-noted glow of paintings on white lead and varnish and the luminosity of light passing through stained glass windows, she treats in detail the psychiatric employment of color and expands into a fresh notation of the eroticization of death and death-like states, supernatural terrors, and madness.

Chapter Three is the most triumphant of Dr. Glanville's studies of *Maud*. Although Tennyson himself supplied the designation of his "little *Hamlet*," few critics have examined the claim with serious attention or thorough scrutiny. Thomas P. Harrison clearly preferred a comparison with either *Romeo and Juliet* or *King Lear*. Glanville offers an exhaustive exploration of the two tragedies in terms of seminal relationships: female love and madness, international jingoism and civil war, nature which is "red in tooth and claw, fickle fortune, and an indifferent God."

Both Hamlet and the narrator of *Maud* play at madness and experience the real thing. Both heroes are haunted by father-figures from the tomb with assignments to their scions impossible to fulfill. Both have women to whom they are passionately attracted but whom they suspect of being major impediments to filial obedience. Thus, their treatments of Ophelia and Maud are strikingly similar. Madness and war are related by both to the civil war within and to the religious tumult of their age. The beauty and pride of heroines is strangely parallel with the corruption of humanity and an irresponsible deity. Genetics is the implacable foe of Gertrude and Ophelia: "May Queens ruling a corrupt Eden," and Maud: daughter to an "old gray wolf" and sister to an "Assyrian bull."

By the heroes' resistance to Ophelia and Maud, the heroines are turned into victims and the universe is revealed as cruel and destructive. Thus, Hamlet's games with murder become the seed of civil war and the narrator of *Maud*'s inner experience of division becomes the justification of the Crimean War. Just as Hamlet and Horatio are the segments of one fragmented self, Tennyson brings to hearing the antiphonal voices of *Maud*'s narrator. As Dr. Glanville sums it up: "Through the efforts of two of the world's most accomplished and talented writers, what unfolds before us is a tragedy of lofty idealism at war with 'a wretched race' and with itself."

As an enthusiastic and practical teacher and scholar, the author concludes her study by providing her students and readers with a comprehensive and useful annotated bibliography of *Maud* scholarship.

Elton E. Smith
Distinguished Professor of British Literature and the Bible
University of South Florida

Acknowledgments

As *Maud* remains marginally represented in the corpus of Tennyson scholarship, I think it particularly important to acknowledge those individuals whose wisdom and support proved essential to the completion of this study. To dear friends and colleagues at the University of South Florida, thank you so much for having the vision and wisdom to support this undertaking. The fact that you recognized the necessity of a thorough study of *Maud* is but one sign of your idealism and dedication to meaningful scholarship. I would also like to acknowledge the contribution of Timothy Hilton, Edgar Shannon, Tony Harrison, Susan Shatto, Linda Hughes, Elton Smith, and Kirk Beetz. The scholarship of the aforementioned alternately inspired, complicated, and proved essential to my study of Tennyson's monodrama.

Introduction

This study is designed to explore the major literary and cultural influences that gave life to, and informed the reception of, the work Tennyson considered the zenith of his remarkable poetic career: *Maud*. Such an exploration necessitates a study of this length and nature, for within the ever increasing corpus of Tennyson scholarship, the poet's own favorite work continues to be shamefully under-represented. A clear product of both the Romantic sensibility and the Victorian social and religious framework, it takes a central position in the critical studies of neither. Thus, the following study examines, in-depth, *Maud*'s largely ignored relationship with the work Tennyson himself cited as its ancestor: Shakespeare's *Hamlet*: its relationship with the Spasmodic closet dramas to which it has been most unfortunately and detrimentally linked; and with Pre-Raphaelitism: an artistic movement Tennyson is often credited with having inspired but never recognized as having mastered. In addition to such examinations, it presents an annotated bibliography of *Maud* scholarship, from 1855 to the present, with the intent of facilitating future research.

From 1855 forward, critics have maligned *Maud* for adopting the language, form, and theme of its supposed Spasmodic ancestors. Nevertheless, such associations quickly dissolve under careful scrutiny. For example, *Maud* examines the relationship between love, madness, and social responsibility, and, in doing so, it features an innocent yet unstable hero who is sacrificed to a grossly immoral age. In comparison, the Spasmodic closet dramas have as a central theme the redemption of young men who gorge themselves on violence or pleasure in order to gain the experience they will need to lead their age morally and artistically. Most of them are ironic mockeries of the Shelleyan prophet-poet who are nevertheless redeemed and embraced by God. The narrator of *Maud* sees the poet as foolish and corrupt, and he sees God and the church as indifferent and cruel promoters of violence, lovelessness, false beauty, pride, and greed. While the Spasmodic narrators alternate between fragments (i.e. spasms) and long, tiresome poetic flights full of the most absurd conceits imaginable, Tennyson's hero speaks in rhythms appropriate for his emotional states and patterns that reveal the disassociation of ideas common to the insane. Unfortunately, a shared influence of the Romantic hero led critics to dismiss *Maud* because of superficial similarities that were present in Tennyson's work long before 1855. Even more horrific, they saw the narrator's faults and instabilities as a blueprint into the poet's own psyche, in spite of Tennyson's multiple rejections of this relationship. *Maud* is no more Tennyson's personal monument than it is one to the Spasmodic poets.

In recent years, criticism has recognized that the sensuality and detail of Tennyson's poetry of 1830 through 1833 influenced the development of the Pre-Raphaelite movement. However, such discussions fall short of a thorough analysis of the Pre-Raphaelite conventions in Tennyson's own work, and they entirely overlook the possibility that this phase of Tennyson's poetic talent reached its height with the publication of his infamous monodrama. Hence, this work seeks to highlight the Pre-Raphaelite conventions of Tennyson's own work, focusing on "Mariana," "The Lady of Shalott," and, with particular emphasis, *Maud*. For example, in "Mariana" and in *Maud*, the Pre-Raphaelite potpourri of tiny objects becomes a phantasmagoric tapestry of vivid, hyper-realistic hallucinations. In *Maud* and in "The Lady of Shalott," the use of color guides the reader through the subject's fall into ruin as it guides a viewer's eye over the prominent features of a Pre-Raphaelite painting. All three of the works in question epitomize the Pre-Raphaelite obsession with trances, dreams, and the supernatural--and the attendant conjunction between death and eroticism. Some attention is also directed toward the hero of *Maud*'s retreat into myth, for his love interest is alternately his Venus, Mary, Diana, or Proserpina, and he her Adonis, idolater, or Endymion. Through close analysis of the thematic and technical characteristics of Tennyson's poems, and of the paintings of the Pre-Raphaelite brotherhood, we find that Tennyson was not only a mentor to the young band of iconoclasts but a master of their medium.

2

Chapter Three treats Tennyson's assertion that *Maud* is "a little *Hamlet*" by exploring the monodrama as a Victorian adaptation of Shakespeare's work, with antiphonal voices taking the roles of Hamlet, Laertes, and, to a lesser degree, Horatio. It should be noted that Tennyson himself linked *Maud* to *Hamlet* on at least two occasions, and his earlier "Ulysses" reveals his sense that *Hamlet* contains themes equally relevant to Victorian England. For example, consider the wealth of similarities between the two works: a culture beset by civil war with actual war looming in the background, a hero who loses his parents to "lust of gain in the spirit of Cain" (*Maud* I.23) and his sanity to terrors inspired by love. In both cases, the love interest is tainted by, and sacrificed to, the sins of others, for both Maud and Ophelia are seen as "painted faces" who wear familial stains and weave snares for their victims. Both dramas are inundated with images of nature "red in tooth and claw," of a jungle constructed on Darwinism and Social Darwinism under the gaze of an indifferent God. Both conclude with the hero's undoing by the Civil War he raged against when sane and championed after his fall into madness. Indeed, the statement with which Shakespeare's drama concludes: "Such a sight as this / Becomes the field but here shows much amiss," could be perceived as the central theme of *Maud*. Tennyson said as much when he refuted the supposed jingoistic undertones of his monodrama. In penning *Maud*, Tennyson was not championing violence and brutality on the battlefield so much as he was showing how monstrously out of place they are at the hearth.

Chapter Four introduces the body of *Maud* scholarship from 1855 to the present day. Most of the entries briefly note focal points of the works in question, and the degree to which each entry is annotated is contingent upon that work's unique contribution to scholarship or, occasionally, by the availability of resources. Unpublished dissertations and, to a lesser degree, theses, are included in this compilation. To ignore the often wonderful work of junior scholars would be to uphold the same exclusivity this study is designed to combat.

Chapter One

Maud and the Spasmodic Closet Dramas

In 1868, in a representative estimate of Spasmodicism, James Smetham added a
voice to the cacophony:

> Don't you remember that just when you were shedding your mere youth
> and entering the golden age . . . there appeared what was considered a
> starry group of poets, soon and most fairly obscured as the Spasmodic
> school? Alexander Smith, Sydney Dobell, Phillip Bailey, I can't say I
> was ever carried off my feet by them. I used to dislike the *Balder* tone
> considerably, and the only book I ever flung to the other side of the
> room was *Festus.* (qtd. in Cruse 180)

As a great American Modernist once noted, "It is invariably saddening to look

through new eyes at things upon which you have expended your own powers of

adjustment" (Fitzgerald 101). Nevertheless, in this modern age of intellectual

prowess, sophisticated readers are more than adaptable to a fresh perspective, more

than able to look through new eyes and evaluate their own analysis. Why, then, do

we continue to associate Tennyson, a cautious and meticulous stylist, with an

infamously shocking and notoriously random school of poetry? Are we, like many

of *Maud*'s Victorian detractors, celebrating the Romantic strains of Tennyson's

poetry of the 1830s yet dismissing as Spasmodic those same qualities when they

surface in his monodrama of the 1850s? Are we inclined to judge as extravagantly

morbid or injudicious *Maud*'s frank presentation of madness and Victorian social ills? Even worse, are we inclined to take for granted *Maud*'s supposed Spasmodic ancestry, peppering our work with the label, often without sharing our justification for having done so? As Edgar Shannon confirmed in his 1953 survey of *Maud*'s critical reception, the monodrama was initially subjected to the most bitter denunciation of Tennyson's literary career (398). The most scathing among the work's early detractors were those critics who linked the work, stylistically and thematically, to the closet dramas of the early Victorian poets known as the Spasmodics. Prominent twentieth century critics proved equally likely to denounce supposed similarities between Tennyson's *Maud* and the works of the three major Spasmodic poets: Phillip Bailey, Alexander Smith, and Sydney Dobell. Through a close scrutiny of the works in question, the often touted similarities quickly disintegrate. Nevertheless, the label, explicitly justified or otherwise, remains very much at large in current scholarship.

Spasmodicism was first defined and first publicly attacked in 1854, when William Edmondstoune Aytoun published a mock Spasmodic drama, *Firmilian, or the Student of Badajoz: a Spasmodic Tragedy*. Attributed to a dramatist named T. Percy Jones, Aytoun's satire parodies the work of a few working class poets of the late 1830s through the mid 1850s. These poets constructed characters around exaggerated Byronic narcissism and an ironic self-perceived calling as Shelleyan prophet-poets. In the preface to *Firmilian*, Jones briefly introduces the shared technical characteristics of such writers, whom he labels "the Spasmodic school" (vii). Jones then concedes that he applies the label Spasmodic to the subtitle of his own work but does so merely to prove that he does not "stand in terror of a nickname" (vii). In May of 1854, Aytoun reviewed his forthcoming production for an edition of *Blackwood's Edinburgh Magazine*. In this review, he praises Jones as the most accomplished of the "offensive swaggering . . . rhymsters" known as the Spasmodics, a band of writers whose poetic stylings he compares to "a beer bottle voiding its cork, and spontaneously ejecting its contents right and left" (Review of *Firmilian* 534).

6

Firmilian parodies a poetic style in which irregularity of form and indifference toward plot and characterization are presented as the manifestation of Divine will. Often a jumble of strained conceits, obscure imagery, convoluted and seemingly unending blank verse, and abrupt interrupting outbursts, Spasmodic poetry is viewed by many critics as careless in presentation.[1] As Buckley suggests in *The Victorian Temper*: "the Spasmodic poets neglected overall theme and action to magnify isolated emotions, to embroider random sentiments often quite irrelevant to the given mood" (42). Such self-absorption was presumably intended to "champion a faith in the poet's mission, and the sanctity of a subjective impulse as the work of God" (*The Victorian Temper* 62). With this in mind, I find it curious that God's subjective impulses would be embellished with the abundance of grotesque imagery and frank eroticism that, to use Joseph Collins' wonderful phrase: "sent Victorian critics into ecstasies of revulsion" ("Tennyson and the Spasmodics" 25).

Spasmodic protagonists see themselves as voicing the will of God, an entity who apparently prefers representation through what Aytoun and other critics describe as "unintelligible ravings" (Review of *Firmilian* 534). A self-worshiping poet who sees himself as representing divinity on Earth, the Spasmodic hero thus makes a mockery of the lofty Shelleyan prophet-poet. Each Spasmodic work traces the temptation and gross indulgence of such a poet hero, whose sins are eventually forgiven by an extremely indulgent God. Nevertheless, as Victorian scholars frequently affirm, the Spasmodic dramas reveal surprisingly sparse attention toward the creation of dramatic tension or the development of plot. As James Cunningham aptly notes, the Spasmodic drama is not devised around a core of plot and characterization; rather, it is "written for the poetic flashes and the asides on religious matters" ("The Spasmodic School of Poetry" 5). Such asides and flashes are likewise inattentive to the development of character, for the poet hero's speeches are often stylistically interchangeable with those of less enlightened characters.

After having thoroughly satirized its defining features, Aytoun concluded his relationship with Spasmodicism and re-directed his attention to the crafting of Ballads. According to Cunningham, later "uncomplimentary" reviews of Spasmodic

7

works were erroneously attributed to Aytoun primarily "because they were unsigned" (40). Nevertheless, as Cunningham and other critics have noted, Aytoun's mock drama was so effective a satire of the Spasmodic closet dramas that its popularity heralded an ironic conclusion to the movement as a whole.

According to Tennyson's son, the poet met Sydney Dobell in 1852 during a visit to Rashdall, the much admired clergyman of Malvern with whom he went to college (H. Tennyson 1: 355), and Dr. Ker, brother-in-law to Mary Tennyson, informed Hallam that Dobell spent a considerable amount of time with the poet. Ker also noted: "that he was no commonplace poet your father heartily allowed" (qtd. in H. Tennyson 1: 264). In "Tennyson Praises the Spasmodics: A Second Conversation with the Scottish Mr. Mitchell," Hagen describes an October of 1857 conversation in which Tennyson spoke "in laudatory terms" of Alexander Smith (75). Moreover, Hallam affirms that Tennyson considered Smith to be a poet having "plenty of promise" (qtd. in H. Tennyson 1: 468). It is not surprising that Tennyson, for whom faith was a defining artistic issue, would find "plenty of promise" in, or use "laudatory terms" to speak of, Alexander Smith. Much of Tennyson's work reflects his desire to embrace absolute faith and reconcile that faith with scientific progress. Thus, it seems quite logical that Tennyson would find reassuring the intervention of Divine will that supposedly guides the redemption and salvation of the Spasmodic hero. However, we cannot mistake a suggestion of potential for unqualified praise, nor can we breach the gap between praise and unqualified influence.

Such subtleties did not stop *The Irish Quarterly Review* from publishing a scathing September of 1855 review, which accuses *Maud* of "weak affectations" and affirms: " . . . if this *Maud*, or any other poem contained in this volume, is to be considered as the latest specimen of the Laureate's style, readers will quickly discover the fancy and imagery of Alexander Smith" (455). Nor did it stop Margaret Oliphant from describing the poets in question as a family, with Tennyson "the eldest of the group," Dobell "the sulky boy," and Smith, "the younger brother, desperately bent on being even with the first born" ("Modern" 136). In later years, Buckley's *The Victorian Temper* added to these suggestions that *Maud*'s emotion, form, theme, and substance "recalled the more ambitious efforts of Smith and Dobell," and its hero "lived largely in the same world of delirious fancy that produced Walter and Balder" (63). Because Buckley's work provides one of the more thorough published discussions on the now obscure Spasmodics, his criticism has played a large part in validating and sustaining the idea that *Maud* is a Spasmodic work. In actuality, *Maud* bears little similarity, in form, theme, or substance, to the Spasmodic closet dramas.

In 1843, Alexander Smith published *A Life Drama*: his major work and the Spasmodic drama most commonly associated with *Maud*. In substance, theme, and form, *A Life Drama* is typical Spasmodicism. Here we find the tale of Walter, a poet-hero with an elevated estimate of his poetic calling and an overly robust sexuality. When the poem opens, we meet Walter pacing in an antique room at Midnight. Reading aloud from a manuscript he soon destroys, Walter speaks of his pre-destined mission to "out-roll a lay / Whose melody will haunt the world for aye / Charming it onward on its golden way" (6). He claims that, as the moon fills the night sky, he will "broaden on the skies of fame," for fame is the "next grandest word to God" (9). In the second scene, a nameless lady and her fawn wake Walter from a melancholic slumber in the woods. He shares with her his vision of himself as a poet who "shall hallow Poetry to God / and to its own high use" as he rides its chariot: "The grandest chariot wherein king-thoughts ride" and maintains a firm hold on "the sword of song" (24). He shares with her his intention to craft a poetic masterpiece that will open with "the soliloquy with which God broke / The silence of the dead eternities," pervade "the splendid-mooned and jewelled night" as the "loveliest" words "born of God"(34), and end "With God and Silence! / When the great universe subsides in God" (35). According to Hallam Tennyson, his father found much fault in Smith's portrait of the poet as a seeker of fame. Tennyson's suggestion that Smith "has plenty of promise" was actually succeeded by the following detractor:

> . . . but he must learn a different creed to that he preaches in those
> lines beginning 'Fame, fame, thou art next to God.' Next to God– next
> to the Devil say I. Fame might be worth having if it helped us to do
> good to a single mortal, but what is it? [only] the pleasure of hearing
> oneself talked of up and down the street. (qtd. in H. Tennyson 1: 468)

Tennyson's reaction is hardly surprising, given the fact that it took becoming Poet Laureate for him to forgive Byron for being Byronic.

Walter returns to his antique room and contemplates the poem with which he will earn her esteem "As an old mountain lifts its martyr's cairn / Into the pure sight of the holy heavens (37). However, when they next meet, he shares with her a saucy tale of a young poet's lust. Walter's protagonist is a "dark Page" who tells his love interest that "the devil fisheth best for the souls of men / When his hook is baited with a lovely limb," mourns beauty's chafing of the "greatest manhoods," and speaks of "Sages, with passions held in leash like hounds" (60). When the lady informs Walter of her forthcoming marriage and anticipated early death, Walter simply projects his desire onto the "passion-panting sea" that "Watches the unveiled beauty of the stars / Like a great hungry soul" (71) and is guilty of "toying with the shore, his wedded bride" (90). According to the poet's son, Tennyson responded that "Wordsworth was justified in saying 'The moon looked round her when the heavens were bare' but Smith, 'a poet of considerable promise,' went too far when he spoke of 'the wave, a bride wooing the shore'"(qtd. in H. Tennyson 2: 73). Walter eases the chafing of his own manhood by seducing his friend's daughter, Violet, whom he then discards.

In form, *A Life Drama* is a Spasmodic prototype. For example, many of Walter's outbursts and conceits are barely relevant to the section of the poem in which they are housed. Many of them surface as obscure, absurd, or distracting interruptions in the poem's sparse plot. A walk down a rural lane inspires Walter's description of the "passion-panting sea" (71) and tribute to Night, who rides a chariot pulled "by winged swimming steeds" and cradles in her lap a "drowsy-lidded" Sleep who has "a Brainful of dreams, as summer-hive with bees" (70). Moreover, his words are nearly interchangeable with those of other characters. Like Walter before him, Edward claims that he "would pervade humanity" and "creep into the lost and ruined hearts / Of sinful women dying in the streets" (91-92). As a typical Spasmodic, Walter is eventually rehabilitated. Indeed, it could be said that he progresses from the naughty exploits we expect of a Byron to the didacticism we expect, and are often

10

less delighted to find, in a Carlyle. At the conclusion of the poem, trading silk for hair, Walter re-dedicates himself to the poetic expression of God's will and closes the drama with a Spasmodic mantra:

> Duty stood like an angel in my path,
> . . . Great duties are before me and great songs,
> And whether crowned or crownless when I fall,
> It matters not, so as God's work is done. (158-59)

Thus, *A Life Drama* follows the Spasmodic cyclical form; the poet-hero passes through trail and purgation to confirm his place as one of the elect.

Regardless, critics insist that *Maud*, Tennyson's personal favorite among his works, was influenced by Smith's tangle of erring saints, carnal harbors, and chafed manhoods. One amid the few who disagree, Collins aptly proposes that *Maud*'s creator never finished reading Smith's poem. As Collins notes, Tennyson's recommendation that Smith "learn a different creed than that which he teaches in the opening section of the poem: 'Fame fame, thou art next to God,' suggests that he didn't read, or somehow misunderstood, Walter's path to enlightenment" (27). Moreover, Buckley notes that, following Tennyson's critique, George Gilfillan, the former champion of Alexander Smith, told Sydney Dobell that "Smith should burn his Tennyson and his Keats . . . let him advance to nobler models" (qtd. in *The Victorian Temper* 52).

In 1861, when Smith published *Edwin of Diera*, many critics spoke out against what they saw as his inferior imitation of Tennyson's *Idylls of the King.* Smith had completed his Arthurian tale in 1857, but this fact was largely ignored. His response was a swan song to the poetic phase of his career. Smith noted in *Dreamthorpe:* "Shall I write verses? I am not likely to surpass Mr. Tennyson or Mr. Browning in that walk" and responded to his own rhetorical question with "No, no; let me enjoy Mr. Tennyson's verse, and the blackbird's song, and the colors of the sunrise, but do not let me elevate them" (248). In an 1866 essay for the *Argosy*, Smith, then building a solid reputation as a literary critic, provides his sole commentary on the group of poets "of which Dobell was, by far, the most important member"("Sydney Dobell" 318). Interestingly, he attempts to vindicate the author of *Balder* by extolling the same virtues of the prophet poet that are presented as license for gross self-indulgence, and thus rendered absurd, in the typical Spasmodic drama.

Bailey's *Festus* offers another example of what David Latane, in *Victorian Britain: An Encyclopedia,* calls "overblown Romanticism and a comforting message about salvation" (358). Greta A. Black, in *"Bailey's Debt to Goethe's Faust,"* is less generous, describing *Festus* "full of bad Christianity and bad grammar" (166). Even more damaging, *Blackwood's Magazine*'s 1850 review of *Festus* calls it "a mere farrago of distracted metaphors, and crude metaphysics, and bewildering theology" in which "reason and imagination both run riot together" and "the logic is as insane as the maniac fancy that is dancing with its flaring torch about it" (416). Bailey's "farrago" is indeed a bloodied Spasmodic pastiche of Faustian conventions. Goethe's *Faust* begins with an alchemists's desire to uncover the secrets of Naturphilosophie and subsequent pact with Mephistopheles, while Bailey's drama opens with a pact between God and Lucifer, a pact in which God grants permission for Festus to be tempted and reminds to Lucifer that sin has no real power over the youth, who belongs to Heaven. Right from the onset, *Festus* is marked a typical Spasmodic jaunt through sin to eventual salvation.

Like Walter, Festus sees poetry as "the toil Divine of verse, / Which, like a burning bush, doth guest a god" and as "fragments of the undeemed tongues of Heaven" (229-30). In this case, Festus clearly voices the sentiments of Bailey, who, in the "Proem," describes poetry as "itself a thing of God," for God "made His prophets poets: and the more / We feel of poesie do we become / Like God in love and power, -under- makers" (10). Bailey labels fiction " a higher end / Than fact" and a "higher, ampler Heaven than that wherein / The nations sun themselves"(11). Therefore, he affirms, "'Tis the bard's aim to show the mind-made world / Without; within, how the soul stands with God, / And the unseen realities about us" (14).

Festus is full of the eroticism, graphic imagery, and strained conceits common to Spasmodicism. A typical Spasmodic hero, Festus doesn't need much prodding toward a life of debauchery, for he "can enjoy / Nought which has not the honied sting of sin; / That wanton whetting of the soul, which, while / It gives a finer keener

12

edge for pleasure/ Wastes more and dulls the sooner" (39). As Festus whets his appetite for pleasure, he collects a potpourri of mistresses. Among those selected are Helen, queen of the fair; Clara, a shadow conscience who occasionally shares with Lucifer a persistence in reminding Festus of his duty to God; Angela, a ghost who scorns Heaven in order to "waft through space"(237) in the arms of a lover; and Elissa, who has prophetic dreams and happens to also be the mistress of Lucifer. Elissa's dream vision of decay features an angry God, who "tore the glory from the Sun's broad brow / And flung the flaming scalp off flat to hell" and concludes with a "long, cold skeleton-scream / Like a trumpet whining through a catacomb" (482). Festus' slight need of temptation is especially convenient for Lucifer, who is thus free to adopt the voice and perspective spread indiscriminately among the drama's characters. As Lucifer offers diatribes on the creation, his fall and that of humanity, the necessity of evil, and the pervasive "eye of God" (83), he clearly does more proselytizing than tempting. He assures Festus that "What men call accident is God's own part / He lets ye work your will– it is His own: / But that ye mean not, know not, He doth" (82) and chides him: "Fye / graceless boy! / Mocking thy Maker with a cast-off prayer!" (43). When Festus mourns that he cannot see God's face, Lucifer assures him that true grace is blinding. When Festus questions the fate of humanity, Lucifer responds with "But I pray, I beg, / Act with some smack of justice to your maker" (92), "Be just to God" / Leave off these airs"(93), and praise of "God's boundless amnesty" (84).

Unlike Goethe's Mephistopheles, Bailey's Lucifer joins his mentee to a final reconciliation with God. In typical Spasmodic fashion, *Festus* concludes with an assertion of Divine will, through which the poet-hero and his demonic mentor are "restored, rebought, rebrought / To Heaven by Him who cast ye forth, your God" (631). As Festus affirms, in the Spasmodic drama, "soul and song begin and end in Heaven" (633). In response to the poem's positive spiritual affirmation, Tennyson warned Edward Fitzgerald that he would find it "a great bore" full of "very grand things" (qtd. in H. Tennyson 1: 234). Nevertheless, as Edmund Gosse notes in *Portraits and Sketches,* the Spasmodics "took *Festus* as a model for their more

13

amorphous pieces" including "Alexander Smith in *A Life Drama* and Sydney Dobell in *Balder*" (91).

As Buckley suggests, "the son of a puritanical father," Sydney Dobell was trained from birth to "probe his soul by introspection and self-catechism," to "respect his own genius," and "to worship his own high predestined calling" (*The Victorian Temper* 53). Dobell believed that the poet's divine calling demanded a rejection of "unnatural patterns of logical thought" and a scorning of "the painful process of reasoning" (qtd. in *The Victorian Temper* 55). Thus, the words of his poet-hero, like those found in the work of Smith and Bailey, are often fragmented in form, and such fits and starts are presented as a manifestation of Divine will.

Balder believes that he is God's chosen representative, an appropriate and pre-destined champion for the "living nations, swaying to and fro," which "Like waves of a great sea that in mid shock / Confound each other, white with foam and fear" and "Roar for a leader" (12). The majority of the drama is dedicated to self-aggrandizing soliloquies; snatches of songs; and excerpts of poems read from manuscripts, most of which Balder employs to tout the beauties of nature and his pre-determined role as its representative poet. For example, Balder notes that he was born to "beget a better world" as "the king of men"(341) and speaks of the earth as taking "a deeper breath" and raising "her swelling bosom nearer Heaven / With expectation (343) of his coming. He affirms that he was destined "to hold the pen of nature when she bent / to send her message to the sons of men" and continues "Oh God! To how great office was I born, / To how proud exaltation came I in / Unquestioned as one comes unto his own" (506). Standing between himself and elected perfection lies only his ignorance of death, as evident in his affirmation: "Till he comes, my perfect manhood lacks" (341). While Balder sings songs about nature and offers diatribes on the lofty role of the poet, his child suffers a vaguely incriminating death and his wife, perhaps driven insane by her husband's self-aggrandizing songs and soliloquies, longs for the same fate. In response, he, "like an Eagle sailing old" with "unwavering wings outspread and wide"(513), stabs her. The drama then closes with Balder mourning his "carrion" pride, which "stinks to be devoured" (533). The only reason *Balder*

14

doesn't follow the cyclical salvation through purgation pattern is the fact that the work remains unfinished. Dobell noted, in a September, 1853 letter to his father:

> Balder is the abstraction of the natural good, temporarily overcome by circumstances; but the legend goes on to say that in after ages Balder shall return transfigured and glorified to restore and bless the world. I propose to call my first book 'Balder: Part the First.' Thus indicating the intention of a second part, in which I hope to develop the idea of the Christian Balder. (*Life and Letters* 1: 295)

For some incomprehensible reason, Dobell, like Smith and Bailey, is often reputed to have influenced Tennyson's *Maud*. Apparently, God spoke, in Spasmodic fits and starts, through the Spasmodics and their poet-heroes, while Tennyson, a deeply religious man, was curiously shunned and forced to compose his own verse with painstaking effort. Even more shocking is the fact that critics insisted, and still insist, on seeing a link between these admittedly random outbursts and *Maud*, the zenith of Tennyson's meticulous and careful employment of meter. One can't help but find it odd that a man who is reputed to have "calculated the sound quality of every word in the English language, except perhaps 'scissors,'" would be given to fits and starts (Eliot, "In Memoriam" 613). Moreover, in *A Life Drama, Balder,* and *Festus,* the protagonists interact with secondary characters, yet the dialogue never seems specific to an individual character. It makes no difference who is speaking in a Spasmodic drama; all characters voice the religious sentiments of their creator. The protagonist's megalomania and delusions of grandeur are likewise diffused and spoken ubiquitously. In Tennyson's poem, the moral apathy of an entire society is internalized, condensed, and released in the quite varied personas, or "pieces," of a character's divided mentality.

Moreover, in direct contrast to Spasmodic fits and starts, *Maud* shows Tennyson's command of language at its most careful and precise. According to Hallam Tennyson, the Poet Laureate stated: "The peculiarity of this poem is that the different phases of passion in one person take the place of different characters" (qtd. in H. Tennyson 1: 396). In the fashion of "The Two Voices," the shifting voices of *Maud* represent the fragments of an ego burdened with melancholy and self-doubt, as they alternately try to fend off the madness inherited through civil war and a father's "black blood." As I shall illustrate in a later chapter, those voices, or "fragments," reveal a Shakespearean birthmark rather than a Spasmodic blot.

The narrator of *Maud*, unlike his Spasmodic peers, is a victim of, rather than the primary emblem of, the madness and moral malaise around him. He reveals his fear of descending into this madness and immorality as he questions: "What! am I raging alone as my father raged in his mood?" (I.53) and "Sooner or later I too may passively take the print / Of the Golden age– why not?" (I.29-30), when he describes himself as having "escaped" Maud "heart-free, with the least little touch of spleen" (I.87), and in his wish: "Be mine a philosopher's life in the quiet woodland ways / Where if I cannot be gay let a passionless peace be my lot" (I.150-51). We must keep in mind the fact that it is not only the speaker's predisposition to melancholy and madness that threaten his sanity and lead to his psychic fragmentation. After all, madness is not solely responsible for his father's suicide in the hollow; rather, the fault lies primarily with the age, an age in which "vast speculation" (I.9) leaves villians "gorged" and their victims "flaccid and drain'd" (I.20): an age in which "lust of gain, in the spirit of Cain" corrupts the hearts of men (I.23). Thus, the speaker's plight epitomizes that of the pre-destined, tragic Shakespearean hero, for, in effect, his fate is a constant struggle to both master his "black blood" and shield himself from the malevolence and madness of his Mammonistic society. Throughout the poem, this struggle is brilliantly rendered in the antiphonal voices of his fragmented psyche, giving birth to a whole cast of characters through this fragmentation.

Melancholy can be the catalyst that leads a wounded psyche to madness, and madness often leads that psyche back to an acute state of melancholy. Thus, as the speaker's fragmented personas move continuously between one state and the other, what is lost in this battle is a stable nexus identity. For example, when the hero's love interest dies, before he embraces soldierhood as a means of self-identification, his ego is thrown into confusion, and the melancholy of the lover gives way to the ravings of a madman. Our speaker envisions himself buried alive, and his speech depicts his lack of a central identity through abrupt changes from subject to subject:

16

> And my heart is a handful of dust,
> And the wheels go over my head,
> And my bones are shaken with pain,
> For into a shallow grave they are thrust,
> Only a yard beneath the street,
> And the hoofs of the horses beat, beat. (II.241-46)

Thus, while Spasmodic madness is conventionally manifested in an over-indulgence in the lust and pleasure common to Walter and Festus, the narrator of *Maud* is literally mad. The Spasmodic heroes' madness is a moral, rather than a mental, malaise and a product of their own making. *Maud*'s narrator is seldom, and then only slightly, self-aware, and his madness results from a biological predisposition to melancholy and a psyche horrified and fragmented by an immoral climate he does not consciously exacerbate.

As Charles Kingsley proposes in *Fraser's Magazine*, "the poem, if taken as a delineation of the path to madness," is "accurate and subtle, and not without use in an age when the madhouses are full" (Review of *Maud* 268). We know that Tennyson visited Matthew Allen's asylum at High Beach; thus, it is not surprising that Tennyson's monodrama carefully imitates the "alternating states of excitement and depression" Dr. Allen described as "symptomatic of insanity" (qtd. in Maudsley 297). As noted in Roger Platizky's dissertation, *Madness and Method in Tennyson's Poetry,* in *Maud*, as in his other poems, Tennyson strives "to paint a realistic, morally ambiguous portrait of madness and not to sentimentalize, satirize, or otherwise trivialize insanity" (195). Thus, the ravings of *Maud's* narrator, although they are often compared to the divinely inspired fits and starts of the Spasmodics, are actually the verbal representation of a psychological loop in which madness and melancholy continuously feed on one another. In this, as in all other details, in direct contrast to Spasmodic fits and starts, Tennyson is careful and precise. An October, 1855 entry in *British Quarterly Review* apparently recognizes *Maud*'s metrical experiments as being successfully and spectacularly original, noting:

> ... as if expressly to mark the poet's intention to shake himself free in
> this poem from all shackles of customary prosody, he has done two
> things far more significant in their nature than merely passing at will

17

from measure to measure, and from one rhythmical combination to another: he has shown a preference throughout the whole poem for verse constructed on what prosodians call the unmetrical principle, that is, for verse in which the syllables are not multiples of the accents; and he has written a considerable part of it in a totally new species of such verse invented by himself for the occasion. (Review of *Maud* 486-87).

London Quarterly Review also addresses this originality, in an October, 1855 review that describes Tennyson as possessing "a high and independent place among the English poets," criticizes "the subjective school of poetry with which Mr. Tennyson is commonly, but not quite fairly, identified" and objects to the comparison of Tennyson's "genuine and original" poem "with what is meretricious and extravagant in his younger rivals" (Review of *Maud* 218-19).

In comparison to the conventional Spasmodic theme, *Maud* bears only superficial similarities and striking incongruities. Tennyson obviously sought God everywhere – in his work, his relationships, in the expectation of an afterlife– yet did he claim to have found this being? Did Tennyson profess to have God's ear? Moreover, did he profess to speak with God's voice? Did he claim that his work served the same lofty purpose as that touted by the Spasmodic poets and their self-lauding heroes? Where Smith and Dobell use their narrators to preach a sermon concerning the lofty and divine position of the poet, Tennyson's poetry often reflects the doubt and yearning that characterize his desire for absolute faith. *Maud*'s protagonist, although guilty of excessive narcissism, never overinflates his self-worth or touts the supremacy of the poet. In fact, he states that the poet, like the scientist, is all too often foolish and corrupt, noting: "The passionate heart of the poet is whirl'd into folly and vice / I would not marvel at either, but keep a temperate brain" (I.140-41). Likewise, he never so much as suggests that he has a special relationship with a God-like entity, power over nature, or the ability to speak for either of them. On the contrary, he sees his life as utterly hopeless and existence itself as meaningless. He states: "I have neither hope nor trust; / May make my heart as a millstone, set my face as a flint / Cheat and be cheated, and die– who knows? We are ashes and dust" (I.30-32). God, to this narrator, is cruel and indifferent, as evident in his statement: "We are puppets,

18

Man in his pride, and Beauty fair in her flower" and his rhetorical question: "Do we move ourselves, or are we moved by an unseen hand at a game / That pushes us off from the board, and others ever succeed?" (I.126-28). His religious pessimism thus reflects that of Shakespeare's Hamlet, who, as we shall later discuss, clearly associates God with injustice and civil war. If not malicious, God's designs are at least unknowable, for the hero affirms "the drift of the maker is dark" and questions "Who knows the ways of the world, how God will bring them about?"(I.143-45). Furthermore, while the Spasmodic heroes are sacred beings whose egotism leads them to alternate between rejection and projection of God's word, the hero of *Maud* curses the world that scorns him and questions humanity's relationship with God, yet he neither curses God nor considers himself God-like or unconditionally elected. As Margaret Oliphant observes, the speaker "does not think himself a divinity; he has not a manuscript to draw forth and gaze upon delighted eyes; he is not– let us be grateful– a poet" ("Modern" 133). In Tennyson's timely and poignant tragedy, God is curiously absent . . . and silent.

Also serving as a contrast to typical Spasmodic conventions, the erotic aspect of *Maud* is developed only so far as to evoke sympathy for the protagonist and reveal his terror of, and fixation with, his own helplessness before beauty. Such fears and terrors are not the end result of his own base actions, as they should have been, and would have been, with Walter and Festus– had either of them cared to examine the immorality of their erotic exploits. The narrator of *Maud* does not indulge in the numerous affairs of Walter and Festus, and his sole love interest serves an entirely different function from those of his Spasmodic peers. The narrator of *Maud*'s fixation with the bloodied lips of the heath and the rosy underlip of Maud, and his haunting dreams of her spirit growing and fading over his bed, serve several important functions in the text. They serve to remind us of the speaker's youth, his virility, and his passionate nature. This helps to explain his inability to embrace the quiet life of the stoic he so covets or to face rationally the injustice of his parents' death and loss of his financial, romantic, and social prospects. Even more significant, the dual fixation with the bloody lips of the heath and Maud's dangerous

19

beauty, rarely expressed in terms explicitly sexual, reveals the speaker's complete sense of helplessness and injury. Because he lives in a world his father bloodied the heath in order to escape, the speaker can't help but be defensive; he can't help but reject anything that has power over him, including both beauty and the part of himself that admires it. He cannot help, as I shall develop in a later chapter, but find in every Mary an Eve, in every act of God the caprice of Fortune, and in every beast his own extinction. However, at the same time, he has been weaned on the promise of the very love he rejects. The effect of such is a psychic fragmentation that sets at odds the part of him that desperately grasps at hope and the part of him that snatches that hope away. In response, while Walter and Festus are blessed with an ultimate salvation they don't quite deserve, Tennyson's hero is sacrificed to the immorality he only embraces when trying at his maddest to subvert it.

One "piece" *of Maud*'s narrator desperately clings to his love object as a sole means of engaging the world that otherwise excludes him. This part of him describes her as "the one bright thing" to save his "yet young life . . . Perhaps from madness, perhaps from crime / Perhaps from a selfish grave" (I.556-59). His obsession with Maud, be she an Eve or a hyacinth girl, therefore mirrors his desire for self-identification the way Tennyson's poetry mirrors his desire to embrace an absolute faith. As affirmed by Alison Pease in "*Maud* and its Discontents," the narrator "desires to restore to himself a fixed identity within a fixed order, in order to escape the chaos that their absence inflicts on his mind" (102). In flagrant opposition to Balder, Walter, and Festus, *Maud's* speaker must find redemption in the possibly cathartic ritual of love– be it the distraction and romantic courtship of a childhood sweetheart, or the distraction and romantic courtship of battle.

He states:

> If Maud were all that she seem'd,
> And her smile had all that I dream'd
> Then the world were not so bitter
> But a smile could make it sweet. (I.281-84)

As ardently as *Maud's* protagonist rejects the guidance of a divine hand (I.127), he worships "her whose gentle will has changed my fate, / And made my life a

20

perfumed altar-flame" (I.620-21). He informs us that as long as her spirit retains a "grain of love" for him, his "dark heart" will nurse a "However weary, a spark of will / Not to be trampled out" (II.100-106). Only when he is denied the possibility of achieving self-identification as Maud's champion does the hero speak of God's concern for humanity. Even then, rather than embracing Christ, he embraces "the Christless code"of his age, an age in which "the churchman fain would kill their church, / As the churches have killed their Christ" (II.265-67). In this, he is akin to Shakespeare's Othello, who, after losing faith in his wife, dedicates himself to the Christless code of the Venetian hegemony– and to Hamlet, who, enraged by the falsity of female love, perverts divine will in the name of service to the divine. As Platizky has suggested:

> Maud serves as the objectification of the speaker's ego ideal– for at times she is described as divine and heroic– qualities that the narrator would like to possess. He attempts to possess these qualities by attaching himself symbiotically to Maud. (*Madness and Method in Tennyson's Poetry*: Diss version 93)

For example, his description of Maud as "faultily faultless, icily regular, splendidly null" (I.82) is a subconscious reflection of his own psychological ideal, as expressed in his earlier musing: "Long have I sigh'd for a calm; God grant I may find it at last!" (I.77). Conversely, it also expresses his terror of finding his defenses erased by the icy indifference of Maud's beauty. Thus, the love interest in Tennyson's poem, a psychological rather than a sexual catalyst, stems from the insecurities of a tortured selfless soul, rather than from the selfishness of a self-aggrandizing Spasmodic soul.

The speaker is justified in fearing the self-effacing effects of Maud's beauty, for as his relationship with her blossoms so does his relationship with the "Golden age" he previously rejected (I.30). Before he sees her as an adult, the speaker feels completely at odds with his brutal age and savage race, loathing most of all the citizen who hisses war on his own hearthstone (I.24). Nevertheless, when the hero is transfixed by Maud's "wild voice," he is moved by a martial song about men who sacrifice their lives for that same age and race (I.174-79). He cannot help but weep– both for himself and for his age– for he cannot help but praise, desire, and be

21

horrified by her. The conflicting frustrations evident in his reaction stem from his fusion of violence and nihilism with love and hope: a fusion of the two idealized states of being he will spend the rest of the drama chasing and falling short of. As he falls deeper in love with Maud, the philosopher part of him is silenced. Another part of him takes over: the part of him that is drawn to the martial trumpet grows increasingly violent and increasingly obsessed with a nihilistic sacrifice to love. Waiting for her arrival in the garden, he states, quite wistfully:

> My heart would hear her and beat
> Were it earth in an earthy bed;
> My dust would hear her and beat,
> Had I lain for a century dead
> Would start and tremble under her feet,
> And blossom in purple and red. (I.916-21)

When Maud dies, he reaches the conclusion that war is not the disease of the age but its necessary cure. He dreams of a jingoistic Maud and, like the soldiers who followed the trumpet call of the golden age, dedicates himself to the service of Mars. As it leads him from obsessed lover to soldier, the love interest in *Maud* is self-defining rather than self-gratifying, and it gives life to many fragmented selves rather than a perversion of one. As Pease aptly notes, the speaker's very namelessness epitomizes his position as a "floating signified in search of a signifier" (107). His love interest makes evident the fact that Tennyson's nameless hero is more the Hamlet and Othello Tennyson likened him to than a Walter, Balder, or Festus.

Concerning the pathetic fallacy that often adds to the supposed chain between *Maud* and the Spasmodics, I propose that this link is equally problematic. In Tennyson's employment, the pathetic fallacy is entirely unlike the Spasmodic use of it to present oneself and one's artistic medium as superior. Tennyson's hero does not think the sun too dim a crown for his enlightened head or imagine the earth sighing for his leadership. Rather, the narrator of *Maud*, as he is led between madness and melancholy by a self-perceived romantic union, judges himself as harshly as "the men of mind," the "viler" and the "underhand" (I.25-9). Unlike the Spasmodic heroes, who take advantage of any opportunity to be sanctimonious, the narrator of

22

Maud never completely disassociates himself from the savage race he loathes, noting instead: "we [humanity] can not be kind to each other here for an hour" (I.129) and: "We are not worthy to Live" (II.48). Thus, as he is mirrored in the landscape, he is exposed with no greater or less scrutiny, no greater or less circumstance than the rest of his Mammonistic age. Like Hamlet and Othello, he is not immune to the diseases that justify his intense misanthropy– although none of the three realize the full extent of their contagion. Moreover, although he seems to be merely pathetic, projecting himself into the landscape like a conventional Spasmodic narcissist, he is actually not so much projecting as internalizing. A young man who is so keenly aware of the perverse moral apathy of his era– a young idealist who is so sensitive, where his elders are blunted, to human treachery– who so intensely mourns the loss of faith and brotherhood: a young man such as this cannot possibly remain unscathed. Thus, as he delves beneath the veneer of peace, he sees and internalizes the violence and depravity of civil war and projects this back into the landscape. Unlike the Spasmodic narrators, he fits David Morse's description of the Romantic hero as the "consequence" but not "the cause" of his predicament; as Morse affirms, he is "always encountered after the incident, like a perennial fifth act Hamlet" (289). It is no wonder that Tennyson criticized Smith's overuse of the pathetic fallacy. Where Smith uses this device to inflate his poet-hero, thus inflating himself, Tennyson uses this device to minimalize his character, presenting instead a virtual filter, a mirror to the doubt and chaos that characterized a changing Victorian landscape. Tennyson himself affirms that *Maud* is the tragedy of "a recklessly morbid poetic soul, under the blighting influence of a recklessly speculative age" (qtd. in Hill, "Introduction" 214). Tennyson's narrator, like his Spasmodic counterparts, is an egotist, but his egocentricity stems from a lack of self-identity, a predisposition to insanity, and the contagion of a diseased age, rather than from megalomania and gross indulgence.

Comparing the endings of *Maud* and the Spasmodic poems presents another deceitful similarity and a certain diversity. As I previously mentioned, Walter reaches enlightenment at the conclusion of *A Life Drama* and gives himself up to the service of humanity. Festus and all those whom he loves are re-united with a loving

23

God. Balder, had the second volume been completed, would have likewise re-donned a halo. Each of the Spasmodic heroes is allowed to complete the circle, to re-embrace faith and re-dedicate himself to divine service. At the end of *Maud,* Tennyson's narrator seems to have found a similar resolve. He states: "It is better to fight for the good than to rail at the ill; / I have felt with my native land, I am one with my kind, / I embrace the purpose of God and the doom assigned" (III.57-59). However, his supposed enlightenment is the bleakest element of the entire poem. After Maud dies, her would-be-lover simply transfers his attention to another mistress. Red lips become red fields, skirts become tent canvas: the glory of battle offers for his violent self the same chimera his hopeful self sought in a childhood sweetheart. His use of the word "embrace" (III.59) clearly demonstrates the fact that he no longer distinguishes between the two. Because the narrator is entirely self-less, because he is merely a filter for the brutality of his age and race, Maud and the Crimean War offer him the same chance at identity, the same distraction, and the same catharsis. As Roy Basler argues in "Tennyson the Psychologist,"the narrator, in choosing to become a soldier, is merely "substituting one form of compulsion neurosis– idealization of war– for another– his obsession with Maud" (121). As Antony Harrison suggests in "Irony in Tennyson's little *Hamlet*":

> In its conclusion, *Maud* operates ironically and presents us with a man who is both a consummate victim and a hero. From a perspective unexplored by most critics *Maud*'s protagonist may be seen as a dupe going to war for a nation whose values he had rightly despised before succumbing to love and madness. (271)

Although he imagines himself to have reached a Shakespearean hamartia, as expressed in the statement: "It is time, O passionate heart and morbid eye, / That old hysterical mock-disease should die" (III.33), the narrator is unaware of the fact that, in his final grasp for self-identity, he legitimizes and champions the golden age he once railed against. His language, in the statement: "Tho many a light shall darken, and many shall weep / For those that are crushed in the clash of jarring claims / Yet God's just wrath shall be wreak'd" (III.43-5), thus poignantly ties him to "Timour-Mammon who grins on a pile of children's bones" (I.46). Thus, when the narrator

24

claims to be "awaked, as it seems, to the better mind" (III.56), the word "seems" erupts as the dying gasp of the part of him that once saw violence as immoral and mourned its own dissent into madness and pathos. Referring to the reliability of the narrator in this closing scene, Tennyson himself states that the speaker, by the end of the poem: "Is not quite sane– a little shattered" (qtd. in Ricks 261). In the place of a hyacinth girl, he embraces the heavy thumbed baker who lightens his loaves, the poison pestler, and the greedy hawker of holy things, making his earlier vision of himself entombed with Maud's father and brother sadly prophetic. At the very last, he indeed finds himself by courting a mistress. His dream of Maud pointing to Mars dissolves in the reality of Proserpina waving a battle flag, yet, instead of achieving catharsis or enlightenment, he has lost all possible hope of redemption. Directly opposing the Spasmodics' positive affirmation, Tennyson's poem ends with the melding of violence and despair to love and hope, rendering human aspirations futile and human passions meaningless.

Victorian Prose and Poetry, edited by Lionel Trilling and Harold Bloom, offers one of the better examples of the critical haze that even today shadows Tennyson's *Maud*. The editors claim that the narrator is "a kind of parody of Tennyson himself" who, at the poem's conclusion, glorifies the Crimean War as he "goes off virtuously to slaughter Russians" (466). Part of this confusion seems to stem from the fact that Tennyson is reputed to have supported the Crimean War. For example, in *The Return to Camelot: Chivalry and the English Gentleman,* Aldershot affirms that he, like Tennyson, "welcomed the Crimean War as a chance for the nation to prove its manliness" (qtd. in Girouard 141). Hallam Tennyson elaborates on the subject when he informs us that "no one loathed war more than he [Tennyson] did," and that "what is commonly called war" in Tennyson's *Maud*, is simply an evil "more easily recognized" than the evil of civil war (H. Tennyson 1: 401). Regardless, Tennyson's support, or lack of support, for the Crimean war is not the issue here, because the still unbalanced narrator who rushes off to enlist is not the literal representation of Tennyson. Tennyson himself addresses the issue in a December 6, 1855 letter to Archer Gurney in which he writes:

> Strictly speaking, I do not see how from the poem I could be
> pronounced with certainty either peace man or war man. How could
> you or anyone suppose that if I had to speak in my own person my own
> opinion of this war or war generally I should have spoken with so little
> moderation. (qtd. in Ricks 261)

Although Tennyson took great delight in reading it aloud, his *Maud* is no more a personal monument than it is one of Alexander Smith.

In actuality, the similarities between *Maud* and the Spasmodic dramas– in form, theme, and substance, are nothing more than the superficial reflections of a shared Romantic heritage. The theme of Tennyson's "Little *Hamlet*" is the influence of melancholy and madness on a rebellion against, and tragic reconciliation with, a morally apathetic society. As far as substance is concerned, Tennyson's narrator never imagines himself a poet, nor does he see himself as possessing a special relationship with God: two of the most essential Spasmodic conventions. Likewise, Tennyson completely avoids the explicit eroticism that sensationalizes the purification of Walter and Festus. Tennyson's form, as always, is careful and precise.

In retrospect, what happened to Tennyson's *Maud*? Why were critics so eager to dismiss *Maud* as a Spasmodic work? What fusion of historical framework and poetic characteristics led *Maud*, upon its initial publication, to be lambasted even more than the Spasmodic works mistakenly tied to it? What debt, if any, does Tennyson owe the Spasmodics? An 1855 article in *Westminster Review* describes *Maud* as: "a bad opera that we should wish to forget" since "its tone is morbid and opens to us the self-revelations of a morbid mind with the cure for this disease being presented as a morbid conception of human relations" ("Belles Lettres" 598). A September 1855 review in *Blackwood's Magazine* describes Tennyson's "proportionately objectionable and unartistic poem" as: "in effect, unhappy, unwholesome, and disagreeable" (314), and one in *The National Review* adds: "If it is to be said that the poem is expressly devoted to the delineation of morbid character, the answer is that a morbid tendency must have guided such a selection of a subject for art, and moreover that the treatment of it is morbid" (390). This review then labels morbidity "a vice" and defines vice as:

> a perverted tendency to take an undue interest, and exaggerate the importance of, particular aspects of things which are such as lie apart from our wholesome, every-day life, the natural bent of our feelings, and the just and regular subjects of our attention. (390)

A reality that will be made explicitly clear in my bibliography, *Maud*'s early reviewers chiefly objected to what they saw as the poem's morbid and immoral portrait of Victorian society. In essence, they were outraged by the fact that the poet who most voiced the sentiments of his age painted a realistic portrait of that age and opted to blacken it with Thackeray's bitumen rather than gloss it over with a Dickensian veneer. Oddly enough, many of the critics who attacked *Maud* for its morbidity, with the next breath, criticized the work for its Spasmodic qualities, even though the Spasmodic works all end with a positive affirmation of salvation and divine will.

The December 1859 edition of *Macmillan's Magazine* appropriately questions the age's response to *Maud*: "Whence, then, comes this evident misunderstanding of the author's purpose in *Maud*? Is it because the drama is laid in our own time, and deals with forms of evil and disease belonging to our own days?" and just as appropriately affirms that the poem is "surely a legitimate conception, and one which may, with perfect propriety, be dramatically presented" ("Quarterly"114-15). The controversy caused by the thematic and stylistic elements of Spasmodicism led to a heightened distaste for what many critics saw as immoral and unconventional aspects of *Maud*, leading them to scorn the messenger and ignore the message. Thus, *Maud* failed to reach its appropriate height in the esteem of Tennyson's reading public because it was published after *Firmilian* had set in motion a critical feeding frenzy directed toward Spasmodicism. A shared Romantic heritage led critics to dismiss *Maud* based on superficial similarities: characteristics that are not essential to Spasmodicism and that were present in Tennyson's work long before he undertook the writing of *Maud*.

Thus, Tennyson and the Spasmodics are alike in their refashioning of the Romantic hero. Their work is characterized by the same focus on solipsism and weltschmerz yet– in form, theme, and substance– with a very different effect. The Spasmodics took the Romantic prophet-poet and made him an elitist undertaking a cyclical and predictable journey, thus tempering their Romanticism with Classicism and rendering both ironic. Little did they know, their own poetry would soon spark another controversy over morality and the social role of literature, a controversy which would send them hurtling toward obscurity and unjustly vilify the poet Laureate's favorite, most ambitious design.

Margaret Oliphant, in the November, 1892, issue of *Blackwood's Edinburgh Magazine* describes:

> ... the sense of betrayal that many Victorians felt on first looking into Tennyson's *Maud:* the passion, the madness, the frenzy, bringing in so many jarring elements, all the vulgar wrongs and injuries of the day gave us a sense of recoil as if we had been betrayed. (758)

However, she also notes how "the fierce and passionate indignation against many evil and ignoble specters" crept its way "into national life" and "led many critics to re-access the political aspects of the monodrama as full of righteous inspiration as the exquisite love tale was of beauty" (759). In the words of Stephen Jay Gould: "An old clichè proclaims that each generation reads great works of literature in a different and distinctive way" and "a primary sign of greatness lies in the intrinsic richness that permits so many changing interpretations" (20). Likewise, the time is ripe for sophisticated readers to look through new eyes at a work of literature far superior to anything attempted by those whom we label Spasmodic, to focus our powers of adjustment on a effort which, however unappreciated by Victorian critics, courageously dared to question without apology and shame without humor. In doing so, we re-discover a unique strain of Victorian Romanticism, a work so complex in design and execution that critics have often misunderstood its heritage. We set to light Tennyson's bleakest and brightest design: a fragmented narcissist for whom there is no redemption, and a metrical eminence to which few poets ascend.

Chapter Two

Tennyson's Pre-Raphaelite Masterpieces

According to William Rossetti's journal entry for October of 1850, earlier that year Tennyson had learned that John Everett Millais was illustrating Coventry Patmore's "The Woodman's Daughter" and expressed the wish that the young painter favor one of his subjects (*P.R.B. Journal* 72). Unknown to the poet, months before he began the Patmore piece, Millais had started sketching his famous depiction of *Mariana*, and William Holman Hunt had starting working on his first sketch for *The Lady of Shalott*. When Edward Moxon published the 1857 volume of Tennyson's poetry, Millais, Hunt, and Dante Gabriel Rossetti contributed twenty-nine of the volume's fifty-four illustrations. As Richard Stein affirms, "no author could have provided a more appropriate context for the Pre-Raphaelite Brotherhood to express their powers as interpretive illustrators" (285). In recent years, a few critics have even gone so far as to suggest that the subjectivity, sensuality, and detail of Tennyson's poetry of 1830 through 1833 essentially invented Pre-Raphaelitism (Lourie 27 and Stein 287). However, for the most part, such discussions do not attempt a thorough analysis of the Pre-Raphaelite conventions in Tennyson's own work and entirely overlook the fact that this phase of Tennyson's poetic talent re-surfaced, in 1855, with the publication of his much-maligned monodrama. As close analysis demonstrates, Tennyson's Pre-Raphaelite phase is manifested, impressively, in "Mariana" and "The Lady of Shalott," and it reaches its zenith in *Maud*.

One quality of Pre-Raphaelitism is its creation of an artistic harmony from a wealth of tiny objects. As Victorian critics often note, this convention seems to foreshadow Darwin's theory of scientific multiplicity– a theory that originated when Darwin excavated a rock and found it an amalgamation of hundreds of shells quite varied in type, form, and size. In Pre-Raphaelite painting and poetry, this notion of scientific multiplicity surfaces as a "precise, almost photographic representation of even humble objects" (Landow). It is this adherence to the precise recording of natural phenomena that the Pre-Raphaelites shared with John Ruskin: the art critic who claimed to understand Pre-Raphaelitism after noting the intricate details of ivy leaves wrapped around a hedgerow (Hilton 15). However, in the works of the Pre-Raphaelites, this attention to the minute particulars of their subjects, and the attendant piling up of sensory detail, often lend the work an otherworldly quality or hyper-realism.

A second convention of Pre-Raphaelite art is its pronounced reliance on color– profuse, varied, and high in value– to achieve its effects. Often, color underscores the painting's composition and guides the viewer's eye through its prominent features. In the early nineteenth century, Romantic paintings were often quite dark in color. This was due to their artists' use of bitumen, a tar-like substance that has a blackening, flattening effect (Hilton 56). The Pre-Raphaelites rejected this convention by painting on canvas that had been lathered with white lead and varnish, thus giving their work a luminous effect similar to that of light passing through a stained glass window (Hilton 56). One peculiarity of Pre-Raphaelite art that particularly antagonized Victorian pundits was the painters' tendency to ignore the conventions of light and shade and illuminate objects without the influence of a visible light source (Hilton 57). This use of color, and re-defining of the laws of light and shadow, enhanced the paintings' phantasmagoric effect.

Millais' *Lorenzo and Isabella* is a fine example of the Pre-Raphaelites' use of luminous color and minute detail. In this work, the placement of bright color leads the viewer's eye around the left side of the painting, from the malice of Isabella's unscrupulous brothers to the ill-fated love toward which it is directed. Note the intricacy of the composition and the high level of its descriptive elements: P.R.B. is carved on the face of a chair, the plates feature a decapitation scene, and the wallpaper and foliage are remarkably detailed. Moreover, each character and object are so heavily outlined that, although realistically painted, they lure the viewer's eye through a surreal pastiche of seemingly disconnected subjects. Such effects combine to make Millais' 1849 masterpiece a prototype of Pre-Raphaelite hyper-realism.[2]

This hyper-realism found appropriate subject matter in the Pre-Raphaelites' fascination with death and death-like states, such as sleep, being mesmerized or entranced, daydreaming, and floating. Such fascination evolved from the Romantic idealization of perpetual youth and beauty into Victorian England's social legitimization of viewing the dead. The lovely German youths who lauded Werther[3] by ending their lives in yellow and blue, the Chattertons felled in the bloom of youth, and the painters who immortalized their beauty paved the way for Victorian mortuary photographs and the prominence of the deathbed scene as a public sphere– one to which a priest bearing the Corpus Christi would often lead a procession of neighbors, friends, relatives, and persons met by chance on the street (Aries 100). Prior to death, the scene was often reserved for the immediate family. However, after the moment of death occurred, the deceased was laid out in his or her best attire for public viewing and, quite often, for photographing. A passage from Queen Victoria's diary, occasioned by a visit to a country cottage to see a drowned child, well reflects the perception of death as a private yet public sphere, such as that of virginity or virtue, which critics have made much of in recent articles on Tennyson's lady poems. The Queen writes:

> . . . on a table in the kitchen, covered with a sheet which they lifted up, lay the poor sweet innocent bairnie, only three years old, a fine plump child, and looking just as though it slept, with quite a pink colour, and very little scratched in its last clothes– with its little hands joined– a most touching sight. I let Beatrice [aged thirteen] see it, and was glad she should see death for the first time in so touching and pleasing a form. (qtd. in Poulson 187)

The merit of the aforementioned sight clearly lies in the incongruity of the dead subject's beauty and youth. Were the expired bairnie less of a Chatterton, the sight of his or her hands clasped, as if in prayer, would no doubt have been significantly less pleasing and more ironic. Moreover, the fact that the youth is described simply as "it" makes poignantly clear the child's objectification through beauty. The ritual of mourning thus becomes one of transference, with every mourner a mythmaker and every martyr a myth.

When the subject of a Pre-Raphaelite painting or poem is a solitary, solipsistic female, her deadened or death-like state is often highly eroticized. Much Pre-Raphaelite work demonstrates a marked affinity for the conjunction of death and desire that, according to Aries, originated with sixteenth-century works presenting the mystic ecstasy of tormented martyrs and acquired heightened aesthetic value at the end of the eighteenth century (100). For example, in Dante Gabriel Rossetti's poem "The Blessed Damozel," we find the tale of a woman who longs to be reunited with her lover. Poignantly, her tale is set in an afterlife full of Romantic longing and lush sensuality. She is adorned by three lilies that are lulled to sleep by the warmth of her breast, and the luminous bars of Heaven are warmed to a glow by the bosom of the maiden they embower. Life without her lover may make a prison of her Heaven, but the very intensity of her passion subdues purity itself– so much so that Mary is envisioned as empathizing with her wasting sexuality. In Christina Rossetti's "Goblin Market," one of the poem's protagonists, Lizzie, is presented as a Christ figure who sacrifices herself to redeem a sister's virtue– and who does so by encouraging ravishment from lascivious, bestial male goblins and then letting her sister lick their juices from her face. Christ's "Drink from it, all of you. This is my blood of the covenant, which is poured out for many for the forgiveness of sins" (Matthew 26: 27-28) surfaces in "Eat me, drink me, love me . . . For your sake I have braved the glen" (471-73) as Lizzie makes of her own lovely face an altar on which on offering is made.

Whether the eroticized subject experiences a rapturous spiritual transformation or catharsis within a dissolving glen, she remains a passive effect of the mythologizing voyeuristic onlooker. As Lionel Lambourne and others have suggested, when caught in a fixed but interpretive altered state, she enjoys social engagement only while distanced from the living world of reality. At the same time, the distanced subject becomes a passive vehicle for the admiration and imagination of a voyeuristic onlooker. In both cases, the living world of reality and fraternity gives way to contact and activity engendered by passive admiration (Lambourne 193). When the stained glass effect adorns the pictorial representation of women embowered by such states, wasting female sensuality becomes a badge of feminine virtue and saintliness. Every Rapunzel becomes a Mary, and every Pandora becomes an Eve.

Rossetti's 1863 masterpiece, *Beata Beatrix,* is an excellent example of the Pre-Raphaelites' obsession with altered, often eroticized states. This famously luminous and infamously sensual painting features Elizabeth Siddal as Dante's Beatrice, dying in a rapture of passion under the approving gaze of Dante and Love. In the foreground of the painting, a bird representing the angel of death offers Beatrice a poppy flower: a symbol of sleep and source of opium, which proved the agent of Siddal's demise. As noted by Hilton and other critics, the look on her face suggests a moment of sexual and religious ecstasy that Rossetti himself refers to when he describes her as "rapt from Earth to Heaven" (qtd. in Hilton 181). Millais' *Ophelia* and Burne-Jones' *The Legend of the Briar Rose* series provide two, among many, additional examples of the eroticization of death and death-like states.

We know that Tennyson held a mutually rewarding relationship with the Pre-Raphaelite Brotherhood and those associated with the Pre-Raphaelite style. For instance, it was upon Tennyson's suggestion that Millais changed the foliage in his famous depiction of Ophelia. The poet even presumed to offer the painter his impression "as to the limits of realism in painting," noting:

> If you have human beings before a wall, the wall ought to be picturesquely painted, and in harmony with the idea pervading the picture, but must not be made obtrusive by the bricks being *too* minutely drawn, since it is the human beings that ought to have real interest for us in a dramatic picture. (qtd. in H. Tennyson 1: 380-81)

Gabriel Rossetti attended a dinner party, held by the Brownings on September 28th, 1855, at which Tennyson recited *Maud.* Rossetti was impressed with the dramatic reading, for he later wrote about it in a letter to William Arlington, in which he described Tennyson as "quite as glorious in his way as Browning in his, and perhaps of the two even more impressive on the whole personality" (qtd. in H. Tennyson 1: 390 n1). In 1860, Tennyson and Thomas Woolner undertook a journey to Tintagel and joined Val Prinsep and Holman Hunt at Penzance (H. Tennyson 1: 460-64). Moreover, it was Burne-Jones who suggested that Tennyson give the name Vivien to the seductive enchantress of Merlin, thus departing from the less morally culpable Nimue of Malory's *Morte D'Arthur*. The poet was held in such high regard by the young idealists that, in 1856, Ruskin, himself a great fan of *Maud*, apparently became concerned with Tennyson's growing influence over them. Ruskin noted:

> I should particularly insist at the present time on the careful choice of subject because the Pre-Raphaelites, taken as a body, have been culpably negligent in this respect, not in humble respect of nature, but in morbid indulgence of their own impressions. They happen to find their fancies caught by a bit of oak hedge, or the weeds at the site of a duck pond, because, perhaps, they remind them of a stanza of Tennyson. (qtd. in Leng 65)

Obviously a relationship existed between Tennyson and the band of young idealists. I am merely suggesting that this bond is as much a technical relationship as it is one of camaraderie and occasional mentorship.

For example, in the poem "Mariana" we visit Tennyson's version of the emblematic Pre-Raphaelite fantasy: a phantasmagoric vision created to illuminate the plight of a eroticized female subject who alternates between sleep, trance, daydream, and other death-like states. As in most Pre-Raphaelite works, a sense of timelessness abounds. Trapped like the insect caught in her molding windowpane, Mariana loathes each sunrise because it changes nothing in her situation. Nevertheless, she refuses to shun her "dreamy house" (61) in favor of the living world beyond the "lonely moated grange" (8). Hers is the fate depicted in Wiliam Holman Hunt's *Isabella and the Pot of Basil*, the slow physical, psychological, and sexual wasting common to Pre-Raphaelite maidens with full lips and low foreheads.

In this poem, emotional syllogisms and hyper-realistic details combine to iconographically illustrate Mariana's madness, a madness most twentieth and twenty-first century feminists attribute to the suppression and inversion of sexual energy.

For example, as the boundaries are blurred between the world of reality and the netherworld of emotional syllogism, Mariana imagines faces passing through doorways and crevices (65-66), feet falling on the upper floors (67), voices calling from outside her window (68), and a poplar tree's wasted wooing of the wind (75). Her home itself is a montage of objects blackened, worn, broken, or rusted (1-6). Her surroundings thus well-reflect the iconographical representation of death through ordinary objects that became widespread in the sixteenth and seventeenth centuries (Aries 192). As hundreds of shells give way to the creation of Darwin's giant rock, the wealth of objects that comprise Mariana's world fossilize her in all but name.

The poem's color symbolism is even more poignant. Where the Pre-Raphaelites use vivid color and underlying plaster to infuse their paintings with light, Tennyson uses the absence of color and an overlay of shadow to enhance the poem's surreal quality. As Mariana's flower pots crust over with thick black moss (1-2), bats flit through the surrounding darkness (17). "Gray- eyed morn" (31) breaks over the sleepy "blackened waters" (38) of the surrounding fen, but Aurora's glory is obscured by a thick paste of dust motes (78). Mariana is separated from the outside world by a filmy white curtain: a veil beneath which she is invisible to the gusty shadow that frolics with the shrill winds outside her window (50-52). Nevertheless, when the surrounding darkness is at its most complete, the promise of Angelo gives way to the shadow of the poplar tree. Amidst the breathy shrieks of the wounded wind, the poplar's shadow passes the veil and suffuses Mariana's waking dream with psychological night (56-57). Mariana thus endures a living death– a death engendered by erotic stagnation and manifested in a public presentation of private imaginative desire. Sighing for a Rumpelstiltskin as she sighs for an Angelo, she finds in his place the wind echoing through the trees and her own voice echoing in the void.

As is typical of Pre-Raphaelite subjects, Mariana alternates between sleep, hallucination, and trance-like states. When darkness entrances the sky itself, she draws the casement- curtain aside and welcomes the nihilism that pervades the dreary "glooming flats" (19-21). In doing so, she follows the advice Tennyson later shared with Emily Sellwood, to whom he wrote: "Annihilated within yourself these two dreams of space and time" (qtd. in H. Tennyson 1: 171). Thus, "Mariana" is a bleak phantasmagoric poem in which the subject comes alive only when the weaver of her story offers up her private suffering for the pleasure of a voyeuristic public.

In Millais' 1851 *Mariana,* the subject appears in a setting that resembles the inside of a Medieval chapel. Captured in a moment of ecstatic longing, she is frozen in an overtly sexual stance before an altar of indifference. The luminescent stained glass windows before her and the vibrant hue of her gown combine with her erotic pose to emphasize the fact that her canonization is purchased with a state of perpetual longing. Note the attention to minute detail in the painting and the resulting surreal quality of the scene. The trappings of the material world, however obsessively attended to, serve merely to inch a subject beyond that world. Tennyson's grange becomes Millais' chapel, and the color washed across Mariana's world served only to enhance the shadows washed over her soul. Thus, Millais' *Mariana,* like Tennyson's "Mariana," presents what Andrew Leng aptly describes as:

> a gothic environment in which the supernatural can be represented
> realistically and understood in terms of the psychology of the
> Victorian erotomaniac heroine, whose abandonment by her beloved
> results in her obsession with him and in vivid hallucinations of his
> presence. (68)

The "Lady of Shalott" is another excellent example of Tennyson's Pre-Raphaelite mode. Like Mariana, the Lady of Shalott is sacrificed to a cruel love and a phantasmagoric fate. As in "Mariana," the surrounding landscape is full of activity, but the subject's immediate setting is the material epitome of living death. Like Mariana, the Lady of Shalott is immobilized– her destiny is fixed. She sits passively weaving in her shadowy tower, far removed from the bustle and whirl of surrounding commerce. The minute details of this poem are thus used to illuminate the contrast between her stagnant existence on the silent isle and the surrounding, characteristically Victorian, landscape. Like Mariana, she sighs for a Rumpelstiltskin, for a lover who will blaze through her world and gild the shadows that render lovelessness an impenetrable black. Like those of Mariana, the lights of this would-be-Heaven are extinguished in an eternal night more familiar than humanity.

36

The use of light and color are equally poignant in this poem, for they symbolize the frenzies and pulses of Camelot that elude the stagnant monochromatic Shalott. While the Lady of Shalott sits in the shadows of her gray tower, red-cloaked market girls (53) and crimson clad pages (58) pass to and from Camelot. Funeral processions pass beneath the towers of Shalott in a clash of music, light, and plumage that mocks the stasis and silence above (66-68). Upon the entrance of Sir Lancelot, on still Shalott, the sun comes "dazzling through the leaves," reflects off of his glowing shield and burnished helmet, and washes the sparkling yellow fields in bronzed flame (75-81). Lancelot's silver bugle shines at his waist as his bridle bells sound his pass through the "blue unclouded weather" (87-91). The inhabitants of Camelot burst across the landscape in assaulting color and activity, while the Lady of Shalott inhabits the monochromatic world of shadow and reflected movement. It is not until she leaves the tower that she adopts a physical, active persona, and then she becomes merely a "gleaming" and "dead pale" (156-57) reflection of the light that suffuses Camelot. A ghastly figure "robed in snowy white" (136), she floats toward "the lighted palace" (164) at Camelot. As Isobel Armstrong notes: "The poem describes a woman who can not come into sexuality or language except by dying" (*Victorian Poetry: Poetry Poetics and Politics* 51). When the weaver leaves her shuttle, when the singer shares with the world a voice once reserved for the reaper, the shadow becomes the ghost and private grief is rendered public by its own sacrifice. Her attempt to stall a death march of sexual and psychological decay only serves to further its progress.

Thus, the Lady of Shalott epitomizes what Gilbert and Gubar describe as: "a memento mori of female helplessness, aesthetic isolation, and virginal vulnerability carried to deadly extremes" (618). She may have been transformed, as Tennyson assured Canon Ainger, "from the region of shadows into that of realities" (qtd. in H. Tennyson 1: 117). However, the transformation is not enough to change the course of her fate, nor is the world she joins capable of recognizing her sacrifice. The fairy of the isle, like Mariana of the moated grange, cannot endure what Bloom describes as her "sensuous prison paradise," yet she cannot survive outside of its confines

(*Victorian Prose and Poetry* 395). Thus, when color and light wash over Shalott, she is transformed from saint to phantasm to passive vehicle for the admiration of both Lancelot and her creator's more than receptive audience.

It is perhaps John William Waterhouse, one of the second generation Pre-Raphaelites, whose is most psychologically faithful to Tennyson's poem. In his 1888 *Lady of Shalott*, the first of his three paintings on the subject, Waterhouse presents the "straining of the east wind" (118) and "raining" of "the low sky"(121) as nature's incipient reaction to the shadowy presence that divides the broad stream. As Tennyson's ill fated maiden makes her way toward the light and color associated with Camelot, she is sacrificed to an ideal that cannot endure the intrusion of her pathos. Perhaps it is Waterhouse who best illustrates the Tennysonian quality Arthur Hallam described as sympathy: the poet's ability to construct themes and characters around a single pervasive sensation.

The zenith of Tennyson's Pre-Raphaelite phase and his darkest phantasmagoric landscape surface in the much maligned monodrama, *Maud*. In this case, instead of an embowered female who is sacrificed to love for the aesthetic delight of the public, we find a young man who is embowered by his own consciousness. Sacrificed to that consciousness, and to the social ills that fragmented it, he inspired little aesthetic bliss in his early readers, for Tennyson's readers found little voyeuristic delight in the guilt his sacrifice implied. Hence, in this poem, instead of the "mourner" making a myth of the victim, we find a young man who makes a myth of himself in order to escape the horrors of the public sphere. Unlike the Spasmodic heroes and very much like Shakespeare's Hamlet, he is rarely conscious of his artistry.

Terrified of being a Mariana, of being jilted by Maud as he was by the world that orphaned him, the narrator of *Maud* constructs a cathartic love through which he hopes to elude the horrors of his unscrupulous age, an age in which molded bread is whitened with chalk and plaster in the foul alleys of London. Unfortunately, like that of Hamlet, his love interest only serves to heighten the avarice he longs to escape and leads him deeper into the moral madness he loathes. Hence, as with "Mariana," the subject's madness erupts in hyper-realistic detail. For example, the speaker recalls the night his father dashed himself down in the hollow as one in which the wind "like a broken worldling wail'd "(I.11). He informs us that the grinding of "villainous center bits" keeps him from being able to sleep at night (I.41-42). When the speaker learns that his childhood companion is soon to return, waves on the bay release his dreamy expectations in enchanted moans and voice his fears in "shipwrecking" roars and "maddened" screams (I.98-99). When he interprets a blush passing over Maud's face as a flash of "foolish pride" (I.117), the speaker imagines the wood behind him as a "world of plunder and prey"in which "the Mayfly is torn by the swallow, the sparrow spear' d by the shrike" (I.124-25). The speaker becomes fixated with the sound of Maud's voice, ringing out over the English green in songs of "Death, and of honor that cannot die"(I.177), and informs us that a raven "ever croaks" at his side (I.246). Nevertheless, the Darwinian raptures of nature are more agreeable than the Social Darwinism of the city, which rings with the clamor of liars, the hissing of gossips, and the buzz of "poisonous flies" (I.151-55). Even more horrific, the speaker's home, "half hid in the gleaming wood" (I.258), is a shadowy tomb through which reverberate the moans of the dead, the "shrieking rush" of wainscot mice, and the "shiver" of dancing leaves (I..259-263). In a moment of lighthearted expectation, the speaker hears "Birds in the high hall garden" call out Maud's name and birds in the wood respond that she is "here, here, here, / In among the lilies" (I..412-23). In *Maud* as in "Mariana," the Pre-Raphaelite fusion of tiny objects becomes a phantasmagoric potpourri of vivid hallucinations.

Tennyson's speaker is not completely unaware of his tendency to read his emotions into nature, for he admits that an overwrought mind will "suddenly strike with a sharper sense / For a shell, or a flower, little things / Which else would have been passed by" (II.111-13). Nevertheless, he continues to view the world almost exclusively through the lens of his emotions. Whether he is wearing rose colored glasses or washing his world in purple pathos, his "reality" is a tribute to the power of the pathetic fallacy given free reign. Therefore, the early detractors of the poem who found offensive its hyper-realistic details and denounced its metrical shifts, its morbid mirroring of social ills, and its so-called jingoistic sentiments, seem to have missed its point. In *Maud*, even more than in most Pre-Raphaelite works, there is no clear boundary between reality and hallucination. Hence, it makes no difference whether or not the vilers are too offensively vile, whether the clash of armies will leaden the loaves of the poor, or whether and Poland and Austria are worth weeping for. *Maud* may be a political, social poem, but its presentation of public disease is filtered through the consciousness of a young man whose wits have been undone by public avarice. The civil war that maddens him may be all too real, but he responds to it impressionistically, providing us with the heightened essence of disease as often as a portrait of it. Tennyson's focus is on the emotions generated by selfishness and avarice, not the avarice itself. Indeed, he is here a Constable as much as he is a Rossetti. His speaker's world is one of hyper-realism, yet the minute details with which it is constructed are not meant to be photographically accurate.

In this poem, color and luminosity guide the reader through the speaker's psychic fragmentation as they guides a viewer's eye over the prominent features of a Pre-Raphaelite painting. For example, as the speaker vacillates between equally impossible egoistic fictions, his love interest vacillates between the role of Mary and that of Eve. A "shining" beauty (I.553), a "pearl" (I.640), a "bright English Lily" (I.738), and a white handed "delight" who glides as "a beam of seventh Heaven" to his side (I.505-509), she can all too quickly become a "snowy-limbed Eve" (I.626) who renders his life a "perfumed altar-flame" (I.644-45). Ultimately, she surfaces as a shadow that "flits" (II.151) before him, a spectral bride in a "cold white robe" who leads him to steal through the city streets in desperation (II.159). The color red is another marker of the speaker's psychological vacillations. When the poem opens, the speaker's family and fortune have been sacrificed to the realm of the red-lipped hollow (I.2), the ghastly red rock (I.111), and the poisoner who pestles his potions beneath crimson lights (I..44). Under more optimistic circumstances, red becomes an agent of the speaker's ecstatic passion. After an evening spent with Maud, the speaker imagines the crimson hue of blushes and roses passing from ship to ship ans washing over the four corners of the earth. "Rosy is the West" and "Rosy is the South" (I.575-76) as emotional syllogisms color the very means of life. Maud herself becomes "Queen lily and rose in one" (I.905). She thus represents both her father's engorged self-interest and the "sweeter blood" of her mother (I.477), fused and nursed to full bloom by the passion of her admirer. When Maud's brother denounces the speaker's hope of a romantic union with her, the sun rises in a blaze of "hell and hate" (II.9-10) and the "red-ribb'd" hollow behind the wood bubbles over with "horrible bellowing echoes (II.24). The sun that rises to herald another day without her is "a dull red ball / Wrapt in drifts of lurid smoke" (II.205-06).

At the poem's bleak conclusion, the narrator trades the passion of the rose for "the blood-red blossom of war" and, "with a heart of fire" (III.53), sails off toward the Crimea. Maud reaches out to him "in a dream from a band of the blessed"(III.10), and the coterie on behalf of which she sends an invitation is that of the age, now rouged and engorged by a father's Mammonism and a lover's passion– a coterie in which "the sweeter blood" of Maud's mother has no place (I.477). As I noted previously, death– both literal death and death-like posturing– often plunges a Pre-Raphaelite subject into an eroticized state. In his admiration of Maud, the speaker finds both erotic phantasm and ego-fulfillment. She maintains, for him, these states in death. Thus, in sailing off to fight in the Crimean war, perhaps to join her eternally, he yet hopes to become the subject of his own imaginative myth.

Maud also epitomizes the Pre-Raphaelite obsession with altered and supernatural states, for its speaker alternates between nightmares of Maud, vivid hallucinatory daydreams of her, and hauntings in which her "ghastly wraith" (II.32) plagues his overwrought brain "with a flitting to and fro" (II.81). For example, when our narrator first dreams of Maud, her "Luminous, gemlike, ghostlike, deathlike" face (I.95) vengefully grows and fades above his bed, forcing him to flees his home in terror of her beauty and his own helplessness before it (I.92-101). Thoughts of her "divine amends" gives him a spark of hope that keeps itself warm in the "heart" of his dreams (I.207), yet this vision of "growing and growing light" quickly burns itself into a heap of ash with the onset of day (I.212). When the evening hours no longer cap his obsession, his waking hours give way to daydreams. While "half in a doze," he recalls wedding arrangements having been made for himself and Maud, yet he is

41

unsure whether the memory is culled from reality or fiction (I.285-96). On one occasion, he daydreams that Maud opens her bedroom window with an intent to glide down the wall to his side (I.509). When he wakes from his daydream, he notes that her "death-white curtains" are drawn and imagines her sleeping "the sleep of death" (I.522-26).

In the second part of the poem, Maud's ghost, akin to a Berliozian idée fixe, relentlessly haunts the speaker. At times it is shadow at his feet (II.39). At the shore of Breton, it flits to and fro before him, leading him to wonder if it be "a juggle born of the brain" (II.90). Relentlessly, Maud's "abiding phantom" calls to him from the woodland meadows of sleep and dissolves with the sullen thunder that shakes the "shuddering dawn" (I.176-95). In one of the poem's best known passages, the speaker, who has been committed to an asylum, imagines himself buried alive in a shallow grave. As the dead drone on in ceaseless chatter around him, the hoofs of horses pound relentlessly on the streets above and the clatter and rumble of the city render impossible his expectation of a peaceful buried life. As other "corpses" babble, gossip, and sob around him, he imagines Maud's ghost standing at his head and describes himself as "a dead man" linked "to a spectral bride" (II.318). When the speaker last dreams of Maud, the entity who "tarries" for him (III.13) directs his attention to the ruddy shield of Mars and his own ever present desire for "the glory of Manhood" (III.31). The speaker dreams of waging war "in defense of the right" (III.19) and wakes with lightened despair. As he adds his voice to a battle cry and rushes off to the Crimea, Maud's "dreary phantom" leaves him at last, yet its flight is toward the north, toward the chaos of battle and "seas of death" (III.36-37). He cannot help but follow. The hero finds in Maud his sole opportunity for a lover's self-identification, and it matters not whether he is sacrificed to her living or spectral self. Like "The Lady of Shalott" and "Mariana," *Maud* epitomizes the Pre-Raphaelite conjunction between death and eroticism.

What is unique to *Maud* is the fact that its hero responds to a love interest by constructing a series of myths around her. At times she is his hyacinth girl: the "one bright thing" to save his "yet young life" from "the wilds of Time / Perhaps from madness, perhaps from crime, / Perhaps from a selfish grave" (I.556-59). In essence, this Maud is a female Arthur, and it is not surprising that the germ of *Maud* was penned in response to the death of Arthur Hallam. Nor is it hard to conclude, as did George Marshall, that this germ may present Tennyson's desire to objectify, and thus come to terms with, his own sense of mourning and loss ("Tennyson's 'Oh! That 'Twere Possible" 228).

Tennyson's hero makes a Goddess of his love interest. She is his "moon faced darling" (I.72), his Diana, yet he tries to fashion her into a Venus, to make himself a watchful Adonis, rather than an accommodating Endymion. As Shakespeare's Adonis scorns the lascivious advances of Venus, Tennyson's hero seeks to escape the lure of Maud's too ripe, too full lips and is terrified by the image of her growing and fading over him in bed (I.88-96). As Adonis scorns Venus in order to hunt the boar that gores him, the narrator of *Maud* finally parts with his lover's vexing spirit as he sets off to join the war that destroys him. In both cases, the sacrifice of the hero is eroticized. Adonis is slain by the boar he leans over to nuzzle, and in Tennyson's poem it is the ghost of his lover that points to Mars and sends the hero off to be sacrificed.

In other instances, Maud becomes the hero's Aurora and he becomes her Tithonus. In the days of their unsullied youth, before the advance of his father's death and her father's culpability, he found in her the promise of eternal love, for "she promised then to be fair" (I.68). Now that Mammonism has marched over England and his financial prospects have been thwarted by the old grey wolf, he cannot escape the fear that she will leave him for another, so he, like Tithonus, makes his Aurora a Janus. As Tithonus irrationally accuses Aurora of carelessly and cruelly granting him immortality, *Maud*'s hero often accuses his love interest of trifling with his affections in order to satisfy her pride. While Tithonus suggests that Aurora maliciously sheds false tears in order to beguile him, the narrator of *Maud* accuses his lady of using her beauty to weave for him a coquettish snare. Also like that of Tithonus, his ultimate response to love is to long for death.

More than any of these, Tennyson's hero is a Narcissus, perpetually longing for his own face in the pool. Because he lacks a clear sense of identity, he constantly strives to achieve signification through other means. Maud herself become the pool, and he seeks in his relationship with her an image of the man who is worthy of her love or the soldier who is worthy of fighting her battles. In Tennyson's most Pre-Raphaelite work, the boundary between the earthly and the otherworldly is breached by the subject as well as his creator. As this subject creates a series of myths around which he constructs a variety of identities, he paints himself as a Werther and a Chatterton and then becomes his own mourner-- voyeuristically admiring the self he constructs in his mind's eye.

In the darkest of Tennyson's phantasmagoric poems, the sacrifice of the embowered man appeared infinitely less aesthetic, and infinitely more horrible, than that of the embowered woman. When the narrator of *Maud* is led by his Venus to join the ranks of Mars, he is sacrificed to and absorbed by the ignorant masses who cross themselves in fear at the sight of the Lady of Shalott, the unscrupulous brothers of Isabella, and the Goblin men peddling their wares. As Herbert Tucker appropriately notes, "When the hero at last donates his body and his intellect in military service to the very interests that have crippled him, the cure is the disease" ("*Maud* and the Doom of Culture" 136).

Nevertheless, as I mentioned previously, the critics who attacked *Maud* for its morbidity also criticized the work for its "Spasmodic" qualities, even though the complete Spasmodic works end in ubiquitous harmony and salvation. In its employment of color, attention to minute detail, and dream-like effects, *Maud* better reflects the tenets of Pre-Raphaelitism than those of Dobell, Smith, or Bailey. The sacrifice of the poem's narcissistic subject seems a response to the request of Rossetti's Blessed Damozel, who seeks her lover's physical, spiritual, and moral death. Like Mariana and Elaine, the narrator of *Maud* falls prey to a phantasmagoric blurring between fantasy and reality and merely hastens the spiritual and psychological death he hopes to escape. Unlike Mariana and the Lady of Shalott, he is able to escape the bower of lovelessness. Nevertheless, when he embraces his

44

lover at the last, he will find that the cape she wears is a ghastly black and red, for the mistress who longs to fold her arms around him answers to the name of Proserpine. The face in the pool is once more washed into nothingness.

Maud may be the poem in which Tennyson put down the harp and picked up the trumpet, but his audience, like that of the dying Lady of Shalott, was not responsive to the novelty of his perspective. Hence, when Rossetti sketched the face of private grief and public sacrifice, when he set to paper the only illustration of Tennyson's most Pre-Raphaelite poem, the face on the page was that of Tennyson himself[4]. Clearly, most nineteenth century artists would not have cared to immortalize a Chatterton whose emaciated face marked every fleshly man fiend, a Mariana who sighed for John Bull, or a Lady of Shallot drawn from the darkness toward a hollow emblazoned with a father's blood. Nevertheless, England's great weaver of words and singer of songs spread a thick layer of bitumen over his dark monodrama. In the most original and most intricate of his Pre-Raphaelite poems, the poet, like his hero, sounds the trumpet for England.

When Tennyson set his considerable talent to the creation of bleak phantasmagoric landscapes, he did so with remarkable, unmatched facility. In the Romantic poems of the Poet Laureate, particularly in *Maud*, the phantasmagoric effects that take on a mystical quality in the works of the Pre-Raphaelite brotherhood appear all the more beautiful, more mellifluous, and more horrific.

Chapter Three
Tennyson's Little *Hamlet*

It is hard for a contemporary reader to imagine how deep a sense of abandonment and hopelessness followed German Naturphilosophie and British geology into the religious psyche of Victorian England. What began as the notion that cave mining could lead us to nature's secret treasure troves and a chimeric search for our golden harmonious past gave way to the reality of our own extinction[5]. Science carved a deep chasm in the religious foundation of the age as the postulations of Johann Rosenmuiller[6] and Charles Lyell[7] reverberated ghastly echoes through the very heart of life and our philosopher's stone turned out to be nothing more than the skull of a cave bear. In addition to this, the age was one in which class jumping was not only condoned but expected, and the rising wealth of the middle class, combined with the falling wealth of the landed gentry, unsettled the social structure and prompted materialism to fill the vacuum left by science. In response, Tennyson, the poet who, perhaps more than anyone, spoke for his age, created in *Maud* the tragedy of an idealist born into a culture diseased by covetousness, avarice, and greed: a culture beset, in effect if not in name, by civil war. *Maud* is indeed the product of its age. However, at the same time, we must not overlook, as most critics have opted to do, the relationship of the monodrama to Shakespeare's *Hamlet*: the work Tennyson himself linked it to, a relationship that builds upon, rather than negates, the cultural canvas upon which Tennyson painted his monodrama.

47

Like Victorian England, Renaissance England was beset by religious turmoil and disorder in the social structure. The work of Copernicus and other scientists challenged the Ptolemaic model of the universe, which, in turn, called into question the Divine Right of Kings. The religious implications of this sent shock waves through the entire social structure, just as geology and Naturphilosophie would do three centuries later. Add to this the fact that monastic lands broken up by Henry VIII were increasingly sold to land speculators and a center of feverish economic activity grew around speculators, a rising mercantile class, and the lawyers who fought their battles, and one finds a social structure clearly at odds with a culture founded on rigid balance and order.

Thus, what better example than that of Shakespeare might Tennyson have followed when he created one of his most timely yet ambitious works? Mann's *Maud Vindicated*, a work Tennyson is likely to have approved before its publication, makes a clear association between *Maud* and the Shakespearean tragedy *Othello* (27-28). We know that Tennyson was also an admirer and close reader of Shakespeare's *Hamlet*, and that he saw in it themes relevant to the Victorian culture, because Tennyson's Ulysses voices the sentiments of Hamlet himself[8]. Moreover, Tennyson explicitly linked the two works: describing *Maud* to his son as "a little *Hamlet*" (qtd. in H. Tennyson 1: 396), and to T.J. Knowles as "slightly akin to Hamlet" (qtd. in Ray 15). Nevertheless, criticism has largely ignored this relationship, opting instead to tout short sighted and sparsely developed associations of *Maud* with the Spasmodic closet dramas. In "Irony in Tennyson's Little Hamlet," Antony Harrison briefly explores a few themes and conventions shared by the two dramas and adds to these a detailed discussion of the forms of irony they employ, yet much more remains to be said. Thomas P. Harrison's "Tennyson's *Maud* and Shakespeare" links *Maud* more to *King Lear* and to *Romeo and Juliet* than to *Hamlet*. Harry Hargrave's brief but important "Shakespearean Parallels in *Maud*" outlines specific ties between the two works: the shared plot of a hero who loses a father and a love interest to greed and scheming, the relationship of Ophelia to Maud, of Polonius and Laertes to her father and brother, and the themes of corruption, honor, suicide, and madness. This

48

study will build upon such ideas and yet take them in another direction. Additionally, it will illustrate how brilliantly the antiphonal voices of *Maud*'s hero actually bring to life the characters Hamlet, Laertes, and Horatio, filtering an entire cast through a single but divided consciousness, and explore the two works' shared dramatization of the relationship between female love and madness, between jingoism and civil war, and between nature, "red in tooth and claw," fickle fortune, and an indifferent God.

Consider, for example, the role played by civil war in the two dramas. The narrator of *Maud* is the victim of "that old man, now lord of the broad estate and the hall, / Dropt off gorged from a scheme that left us flaccid and drain'd" (I.19-20). The old man, Maud's father, is clearly a second generation Claudius, and the "us" is akin to a royal "we," reflecting the loss of both Hamlet and *Maud*'s narrator as the rightful heirs of their fathers' property and the fact that Denmark and England suffer on a grand scale from the type of civil war such theft signifies. As the narrator of *Maud* opens the work by linking the loss of his father and his wealth to his Mammonistic age, Horatio opens *Hamlet* by linking the appearance of the ghost to "some strange eruption to our state" (1.1.69). It is important to examine in great detail the fashion in which the two dramas tie the disease of civil war to the religious turmoil of their creator's ages. What we find, in *Maud* and in *Hamlet*, are heroes who have not the traditional outlet of faith to turn to in times of crisis, heroes who rather associate God and Providence with the very source of their injury.

For example, when he learns that his father was murdered by his uncle and that his mother had been adulterous, Hamlet responds with "O all you host of heaven! O earth! what else?" (1.5.92) seemingly suggesting that God has sent the evil of his father's murder and his mother's betrayal to plague him. His next comment: "And shall I couple hell?" (1.5.93) shows that he at least partly believes that the ghost has been sent to damn his soul, yet he still attributes it to God. Thus, we see that, right from the beginning of the play, Hamlet views the universe, Heaven, and, by implication, God, in terms of strife and destruction. Moreover, Hamlet's spiritual health depends on more than his ability to distinguish between the forces of darkness

49

and those of goodness. He must also find the right balance between submission to divine will and accepting personal and social responsibility. Instead of letting divine will mandate his actions and morality guide their unfolding, Hamlet increasingly oversteps his boundaries and, letting his emotions color his moral standards, reads these moral standards into Providence. Thus, as the play progresses, his religious pessimism changes only in shape, as he alternately sees himself as alienated from, or the agent of, the black designs of Heaven and Providence. For example, after *The Mousetrap* confirms Claudius' guilt and the Queen's innocence and Polonius tells him to go to his mother's closet, Hamlet notes:

> Tis now the very witching time of night,
> When churchyards yawn and hell itself breathes out
> Contagion to this world. Now could I drink hot blood,
> And do such bitter business as the day
> Would quake to look on. Soft, now to my mother.
> O heart, lose not thy nature! Let not ever
> The soul of Nero enter this firm bosom,
> Let me be cruel, not unnatural;
> I will speak daggers to her, but use none. (3.2.367-75)

Significantly, Hamlet's anger is directed more at his mother than at the King, in spite of the fact that he has reason to believe her innocent of his father's murder and the fact that the ghost specifically asked him to leave her to Heaven. Hell breathing from churchyard chasms symbolically represents the perversion of Divine will, for Hamlet, who now has the evidence he claimed to need before her could work Heaven's revenge, must do all he can to not execute his innocent mother instead. Moreover, the fact that he sees the church as the agent through which Hell ascends to disease him shows once again that he sees God and God's works as agents of violence and corruption. Hamlet is rational enough to view bloodlust as diseased and unnatural, but he paradoxically and irrationally attributes it to Heaven and then describes it as a barely controllable force that may overshadow his purpose. Significantly, Hamlet's desire for personal vengeance leads him to postpone the requested execution of his stepfather, who murdered God's chief representative on Earth, yet he moves with rash speed to violent impulses toward his mother and the execution of Polonius, who was most guilty in his meddling and foolishness.

Moreover, in Act 5, Hamlet tells Horatio about the sense of foreboding that led him to uncover Claudius' plot to have him executed in England, and he links this foreboding to Providence. He tells Horatio that "There's a divinity that shapes our ends, / Rough-hew them how we will" (5.2.10-11). However, he then, quite characteristically, contradicts himself by reading his own anger into Providence and twisting Divine will to appease his sense of personal injury. Hamlet describes how he made himself the judge of life and soul and had Rosencrantz and Guildenstern executed in his place– without shriving time. He sees his having done so as Heaven's "ordinant" simply because he happened to have his father's seal in his pocket at the time and was able to conveniently impress the orders (5.2.49). Thus, we once again note that Hamlet reads his own brutality into the forces that shape our end. It is significant that Hamlet, when at his most violent and irrational, describes his actions as shaped by Providence, whereas he spends most of the play agonizing over whether or not he has the right, morally, to act on the ghost's behalf. Like the narrator of *Maud*, Hamlet sees himself as alienated from Heaven, as a chess piece "moved by an unseen hand at a game" (*Maud* I.127), and he reconciles himself with Heaven only in its bloody, vengeful aspects. Thus, when the two heroes embrace God, they embrace what they once saw or yet see as corruption: "the purpose of God and the doom assigned" (*Maud* III.59).

An interesting feature of the two dramas is the relationship they reveal between gender, the black designs of Providence, and civil war. For example, in his relationships with Ophelia and his mother, Hamlet finds himself overcome by the madness he feigns and is consequently consumed by the civil war he rages against. He moves from trying to choose between taking his own life or that of Claudius to finding himself justified in attacking or taking the life of anyone he associates with civil war. Although Hamlet does not murder his mother and is only indirectly responsible for the death of Ophelia, he clearly associates both of them with the civil war that corrupts Denmark. In many ways, he is quite accurate in this assumption, for the women in the play serve as pawns to corruption and often mark the point of Hamlet's passage from playing mad into actual moral and spiritual madness, and when Hamlet is mad, he himself becomes an agent of the civil war he once opposed.

For example, at the beginning of the play, Hamlet addresses God, noting how "stale, flat and unprofitable" he finds "all the uses of this world" (1.2.133-34). He describes the world as "an unweeded garden, / That grows to seed" as "things rank and gross in nature / Possess it merely" (1.2.135-37). He then supports this impression with a harangue about his mother's bestial appetite. Noting how less than two months ago she would hang on her Hyperion "As if increase of appetite had grown / By what it fed on" (1.2.143-45), he rages about how she progressed from a Hyperion to a satyr, "Ere yet the salt of most unrighteous tears / Had left the flushing in her galled eyes" (1.2.154-55). Indeed, with "most wicked speed" she ran "With such dexterity to incestuous sheets" (1.2.156-57) he can only conclude, again to God, that "a beast, that wants discourse of reason / Would have mourn'd longer" (1.2.150-51). This passage is telling in several ways. For example, Hamlet describes his father's feelings for his mother in terms of endearment, noting that he was: "so loving to my mother / That he might not beteem the winds of heaven / Visit her face too roughly" (1.2.140-42). In comparison, he describes his mother's love for his father in terms of appetite, and he suggests that her particular appetite was so voracious that it could not be satisfied with a Hyperion and drew her instead to a satyr. Moreover, with clear misogyny, he links his mother's too fertile appetite to a grossly fertile garden and is obsessed with the thought of his stepfather as the beast who enjoys its poisoned fruit. Thus, we see that, even before he learns of his mother's adultery, Hamlet is irrationally fixated upon corrupt sexuality. Moreover, the fact that he, while speaking to God, links his mother and stepfather to lascivious beasts roaming a rank Eden reflects his sense that the universe is out of balance, linking love to his lack of faith in a just universe ruled by a just God and revealing an obsession with female appetites that will be at the heart of his madness through the rest of the drama.

Consider, for example, the closet scene. When Hamlet goes to his mother's closet after *The Mousetrap*, he is clearly unbalanced. We know that Hamlet is immediately

52

enraged by her presence, for his mother is anxious enough to question whether or not he is going to murder her. When he instead murders Polonius, his response is one of mockery rather than shame, as he lifts the tapestry and bids "farewell" the "wretched, rash, intruding fool" (3.4.31). Immediately dismissing Polonius' death as insignificant, illustrating his ever growing desensitization to injustice and violence, he swiftly resumes his harangue against his mother's appetite. His rebuke of her lust bears vitriolic similarity to that offered by Tennyson's narrator after the murder of Maud's brother: a passage that Tennyson revised before *Maud*'s 1855 publication. Compare Hamlet's comment to "Rebellious Hell":

> If thou canst mutine in a matron's bones,
> To flaming youth let virtue be as wax,
> And melt in her own fire. Proclaim no shame
> When the compulsive ardure gives the charge,
> Since frost itself as actively doth burn,
> And reason panders will. (3.4.82-88)

to Tennyson's speaker's:

> Break forth in earthquake & in storms
> Kill kill the feeble vassals of anger & lust
> That know not how to forgive.
> Strike dead, O God, for we hold thee just,
> The whole weak race of venomous worms,
> That sting each other in the dust.
> We are not fit to live. (II.36-48 qtd. in Shatto 129n1)

Moreover, Hamlet's cavalier treatment of Polonius' body suggests that even if he imagines himself playing mad, he has indeed adopted the moral madness of his surroundings. Like the narrator of *Maud*, he has become a filter for disease. Thus, we see that Hamlet's mother serves as a point of entry from feigned to actual madness, for in thoughts of her and in her presence he is overcome by uncontrollable rage, an obsession with corrupt sexuality, and religious pessimism and corruption. Thoughts of her move him swiftly from over-contemplation to rash action, so she is indeed his perfumed altar flame.

Tennyson's hero also associates love and civil war with corrupt fertility and the black designs of Providence. When the monodrama opens and the speaker is overcome by grief and rage, we see that he, like Hamlet, is reading his emotions into his surroundings. At this point, he is speaking, as Hamlet himself often does, with the voice of the mad Laertes. However, let's put aside the question of character mirroring for a moment and concentrate on what the opening passages reveal about the speaker's understanding of God, Providence, and love. First of all, it is significant that the drama opens with the speaker's declaration: "I hate the dreadful hollow behind the little wood" (I.1) and then justifies his hatred as follows: "It's lips in the field are dabbled with blood-red heath" (I.2). In response, he tells us that whatever Echo is asked, she "answers Death" (I.4.). Peace is then associated with sexual corruption, as she is depicted as presiding over civil war through imagery that calls to mind a drunken orgy and Hamlet's rank garden. Lording over her olive grove, Peace is depicted as "slurring the days gone by" as "the poor are hovell'd and hustled together, each sex like swine" (I.33-34). Thus, we see that the narrator of the monodrama, like Hamlet, first speaks with vitriol directed against a world that he, at least subconsciously, sees in terms of corrupt and bestial sexuality. Moreover, he does so even before he begins to fear the corrupting influence of Maud's beauty, just as Hamlet reveals his mad fixation with his mother's corrupt sexuality even before he learns that she is an adulteress.

Just as Hamlet links God and Providence to civil war and the corruption of female sexuality, the narrator of *Maud* links God to the bloodied lips of the heath, Echo's promise of death, and the drunken revels of Peace. Hamlet's question in response to his mother's adultery: "O all you host of heaven! O earth! what else?" (1.5.93) is mirrored in the narrator of *Maud*'s question: "For there in the ghastly pit long since a body was found, / His who had given me life–O father! O God! was it well?" (I.5-6). Both speakers move from an association of death and sexuality to an initial blaming of God for their situation. Interestingly, the speaker of *Maud*'s address may be looked at in two ways: he could be addressing God and asking whether God found the horrors of death and blood well done, and he could also be asking his father and God whether his birth was well done. Just like Hamlet, he endures a horrid discovery of corruption before the drama opens and, when we first meet him, he expresses the

54

fact that he can see no point in living in a corrupt world in which God's designs mean that the best die and leave the corrupt behind.

As thoughts of Gertrude lead Hamlet to increasing rancor, the narrator of *Maud* recalls how "the shrill-edged shriek" of his mother divided the night after her husband fell and follows, perhaps interrupts, this recollection with the exclamation: "Villainy somewhere! Whose? One says we are villains all" (I.17), moving quickly from a discussion of his mother to thoughts of the civil war that reached its zenith as the old grey wolf "dropped off gorged from a scheme had left us flaccid and drained" (I.20). Interestingly, when he questions: "Would there be sorrow for me? / there was love in the passionate shriek" and then immediately recalls how his father would "rave at the lie and the liar, ah God, as he used to rave" (I.57-60), we see that he is associating himself with his father in light of his mother's love and that from this association immediately follows one between himself and his father's mad ravings. Ironically, this address is offered by the part of him that wants to distance himself from madness but will be unable to because he can not distance himself from love.

In the corrupt Eden of Shakespeare and Tennyson, the sins of one's parents brand whore or madman across the innocent faces of youth. Thus, like that with his mother, Hamlet's relationship with Ophelia is a point of entry into corruption and madness, for the malice he directs at her, and his denial of love for her, are bitter, unjust, and irrational. Moreover, the savageness of his attacks makes evident the fact that he associates her with civil war. In response, he both attacks her and tries to subdue the part of himself that wants to believe in her, and, in doing so, is caught in the swell of blind and desperate rage. For example, one of Hamlet's wildest fits is given center stage in his callous treatment of Ophelia in Act 3. Ophelia incites his anger when she tries to return his letters, but he immediately lashes out so bitterly at her that it seems as if her very presence, like that of his mother, enrages him. At the offer of his letters, he rages at her hysterically, laughing and challenging: "Ha, ha! are you honest?"(3.1.102) and "Are you fair?"(3.1.103), thus questioning her virtue. When she asks him to clarify his meaning, he replies: "if you be honest and fair, your

55

honesty should admit no discourse to your beauty" (3.1.106-07). In other words, were she truly virtuous, her virtue would prohibit anyone from approaching her beauty, as female beauty is a hazard at odds with honesty and decency. It is significant that any sign of betrayal on her part leads him immediately to question her chastity; he obviously not only associates her with the deception and intrigue of civil war, he also, with no evidence for doing so, associates her with his mother's lasciviousness.

Hamlet grows even more cruel and irrational when he tells Ophelia: "I lov'd / you not" (3.1.117-18). If he is trying to present himself as mad with love melancholy, what purpose does it serve for him to tell her that he never loved her? Is he doing so for the mere sake of cruelty and spite? . . . perhaps. Perhaps he is also trying to convince himself that she does not have the power to hurt him. Thus, he is akin to Tennyson's hero, who claims to hate, and tries to escape, his love interest in order to escape the hope he invests in one who may be weaving a coquettish snare for him. When Hamlet lashes out at Ophelia, he lashes out at the part of himself that wants to believe in her honesty and sincerity and, in maintaining faith in these, perhaps believe that innocence and honesty still exist in the world.

It is also significant that her requests for Heaven's assistance seem to enrage him even further. Each time Ophelia asks God to intervene, Hamlet lashes out at her, and at humanity, with increasing malice. For example, in response to his comment that all men are arrant knaves, she cries out: "O, help him, you sweet heavens!" (3.1.133) and he viciously responds that she must get herself to a "nunn'ry," for be she as "chaste as ice" and "pure as snow," he will nevertheless besmirch her reputation (3.1.134-39). Once again, we see that Hamlet, at least sub-consciously, associates Heaven with corrupt female virtue, as evident in the double meaning of "nunn'ry." The interesting thing is that Hamlet probably doesn't see his threat as inappropriate, he probably rationalizes blotting her good name as an act of justice because he sub-consciously needs to employ it as an act of self-defense. We already know that he believes beauty weaves a corrupting snare for its virtuous admirers, and his public declaration of such will help his misanthropic side to validate his impression of this and convince the vulnerable part of himself that he can, and must, avoid the dangers of love. After further attacking Ophelia's virtue throughout the Mousetrap, Hamlet notes how the raven "doth bellow for revenge"(3.2.238-39). The raven does indeed croak for revenge, for it sits at Hamlet's side and never lets him escape the horror of female appetite and the terrible lure of beauty's painted innocence.

In Tennyson's casting, beauty's painted innocence bares a hook that bobs once more to the surface, for as Ophelia is tainted by the sins Hamlet associates with Gertrude and civil war, Maud is tainted by her association with corruption. It is significant that the first time the speaker thinks of her it is to recall how she: "the delight of the village" and "the ringing joy of the hall" was "the moon-faced darling" of his parents and the community (I.70-72). Thus, right from the beginning, she is associated with a community full of rogues, cheats, thieves, and murderers. Because Maud is "the moon faced darling" of the local villains, his immediate response to thoughts of her is "I will bury myself in myself, and the devil may pipe to his own" (I.76). Thus Maud, like Ophelia, is associated with the corruption and civil war that infect the surrounding landscape, the corruption that destroys one's parents, and the corruption that the hero will try to flee but find himself unable to.

Significantly, Tennyson's hero then links the corruption of love and humanity to God. Speaking of Divine will as destructive, he calls humanity "puppets, Man in his pride, and Beauty fair in her flower" and asks: "Do we move ourselves, or are moved by an unseen hand at a game / That pushes us off from the board, and others ever succeed?" (I.126-28). Like Hamlet, he sees beauty and pride as the puppets of corruption and an unjust God. Furthermore, when faced with the possibility of her infidelity, it is to Heaven that he directs his plea that she remain chaste. His plea: "Let the sweet heavens endure, / Not close and darken above me / Before I am quite sure / That there is one to love me" (I.405-08) makes clear the fact that he sees God as responsible for her steadfastness or lack of it. His following comment: "Then let come what come may / To a life that has been so sad, / I shall have had my day

57

(I.409-411) makes equally clear how little of justice and happiness he expects God and Providence to send his way.

As Gertrude and Ophelia are seen as May Queens reigning over a corrupt Eden, so is Maud. Like Ophelia, Maud, as the daughter of an "gray old wolf" (*Maud* I.471) and the sister of an "Assyrian bull" (*Maud* I.233), must, by association, be "a child of deceit" (*Maud* I.473). Moreover, just as Hamlet links the corrupt May Queen to God, the narrator of *Maud* affirms that "the drift of the Maker is dark, an Isis hid by the veil" (I.143-44). Significantly, he sees Isis, the Egyptian Goddess of fertility, as the manifestation of God's designs and, as we already know, he sees this God as capricious at best. Because Maud has become his "perfumed altar-flame . . . Shadowing the snow-limb'd Eve from whom she came" (I.622-26), he has been "brought to understand / A sad astrology, the boundless plan" that makes the stars "tyrants" in their "iron skies" and "Innumerable, pitiless, passionless eyes, / Cold fires, yet with power to burn and brand" a "nothingness into man" (I.633-38). In response, the narrator of *Maud*, like Hamlet, rejects God and Providence and tries, quite futilely, to escape the "cruel madness" and honeyed "poison flowers" of love (*Maud* I.156-57).

Echoes of a Hamlet who would be, but cannot be, a Horatio appear as Tennyson's hero notes: "Long have I sigh'd for a calm; God grant I may find it at last" (I.77) and then answers: "It will never be broken by Maud" for she "has neither savor nor salt, / But a cold and clear cut face" that is "faultily faultless, icily regular, splendidly null" in its "dead perfection" (I.78-83). The voice that associates God with assistance is thus answered by the voice that links God to the corrupting influence of love and wants desperately to convince himself that he can escape that influence "heart-free, with the least little touch of spleen" (I.87). In a similar passage, he asks himself: "wherefore cannot I be / Like things of the season gay, like the bountiful season bland" (I.103-4) and then answers his owns question while inadvertently cataloging his obsessions. The progression of his discussion clearly shows that he associates civil war with the hopelessness of his love interest. Because he is fixated with Maud and using emotional syllogisms to read his emotions into nature, he imagines the sea as "silent sapphire-spangled marriage ring of the land" (I.107). Because he is jealous and terrified at the thought that Maud will find "fatter game on the moor" (I.73), the sea enfolding the land in a marriage is associated with the " gossip, scandal, and spite" that enfold the city, which in turn enfolds such characters as "Jack on his ale-house bench" who has "as many lies as a Czar"(I.108-110). Thoughts of lies and corruption lead him back to thoughts of the red rock that crushed his father and Maud's duplicity by association with her family.

Growing increasingly bitter, he then starts raging against civil war and attributing it to the fact that the universe is cruel and destructive. The fact that his man and his maid are "ever ready to slander and steal" forces him to wear "a hard-set smile, like a stoic, or like / A wiser epicurean" (I.120-22), yet his next statement proves that he is incapable of the stoicism he dons, for he rages that "nature is one with rapine, a harm no preacher can heal" as "The Mayfly is torn by the swallow, the sparrow spear'd by the shrike" and the "whole little wood" around him is "a world of plunder and prey" (I.122-25). When Maud first begins haunting the speaker's dreams, "Breaking a slumber in which all spleenful folly was drown'd," her face: "Pale with the golden beam of an eyelash dead on the cheek" takes revenge "too deep for a transient wrong / Done but in thought" to her beauty and "Luminous, gemlike, ghostlike, deathlike," grows and fades around him until he rises and walks in his "own dark garden ground" amidst "the scream of a madden'd beach dragg'd down by the wave" and the "ghastly glimmer" of Orion sinking "low in his grave" (I.88-101).

As Hamlet adopts madness in his efforts to resist Ophelia and is subsequently overcome by the moral madness of civil war, so is the narrator of *Maud*. Hamlet tries to convince himself that he is immune to the dangers of love by treating those he cares about, especially Ophelia, with increasing cruelty, revealing the fact that he feels himself helpless before the baited hook of love. Similarly, the narrator of *Maud* feels that his sweetheart's "sweetness hardly leaves" him "a choice" but to fall at her feet (I.185-86). Yet, because he is trying not to admit to himself the power she holds over him, he claims to be adoring "Not her, who is neither courtly nor kind, / Not her, not her, but a voice" (I.187-89). He then proves this rejection impossible as he starts reading his sense of helplessness into nature, noting that "the budded peaks of the wood are bow'd / Caught and cuff'd by the gale" (I.194-95). In response, he treats her with cruelty and indifference. When she smiles at him, like Ophelia, she makes her lover "divine amends / For a courtesy not returned" (I.202-03). No doubt she, again like Ophelia, is completely ignorant of the fact that she, guilty through association, is seen as someone who means to weave for her lover "a snare / Of some coquettish deceit" and "entangle him" in it, "To have her lion roll in a silken net / And fawn at a victor's feet" (I.214-19). Interestingly, in both dramas, in the place of divine justice, love itself is presented as having the ability to save one from the very madness it inspires. Consider Gertrude's comment to Ophelia in Act III:

> And for your part, Ophelia, I do wish
> That your good beauties be the happy cause
> Of Hamlet's wildness. So shall I hope your virtues
> Will bring him to his wonted way again,
> To both your honors. (*Hamlet* 3.1.37-41)

This mirrors the fact that the narrator of *Maud*, right up until the point at which he learns of his lover's death, cannot escape the hope:

> . . . she would love me still;
> And as long, O God, as she
> Have a grain of love for me,
> So long, no doubt, no doubt,
> Shall I nurse in my dark heart,
> However weary, a spark of will
> Not to be trampled out. (II.100-105)

Addressing God, the only salvation Tennyson's hero can fathom is derived through the love he often describes as God's corrupt agent. Nevertheless, even this ironic hope is constantly thwarted by the fear and helplessness her beauty inspires in him. For example, at the sight of his "Oread coming down" he foresees that he will "dream of her beauty with tender dread" and further comments: "O, if she knew it / To know her beauty might half undo" the chance of her saving his "yet young life in the wilds of Time, / Perhaps from madness, perhaps from crime, / Perhaps from a selfish grave" (I.544-59). Thus we see that even as he hopes she will prove a hyacinth girl, a part of him accepts the fact that her beauty makes this unlikely if not impossible. Like that of Ophelia, Maud's virtue must allow no discourse to her beauty.

Unfortunately, neither the mad narrator of *Maud* nor the mad Hamlet recognize beauty as anything but at odds with virtue. This association leads Hamlet to have to restrain his murderous impulses toward his mother, and it leads the narrator of *Maud* to ask his "clamorous heart" to "catch not his breath" or let his "tongue be a thrall" to his "eye" before he can speak to Maud and hear her affirm her loyalty to him (I.569-70). As the raven ever croaks for the wary and vulnerable Hamlet, it croaks to remind the narrator of *Maud* to "keep watch and ward, keep watch and ward, / Or thou will prove their tool" (I.246-47). Yet the raven's warning is falser than love and falser than his momentary flash of self-awareness: "myself from myself I guard / For often man's own angry pride / Is cap and bells for a fool" (*Maud* I.249-51). Maud, like Ophelia, is a victim: a silent signifier who is characterized more when filtered through the consciousness of others than in her own words and actions. Both are puppets to relatives, both are guilty of love rather than donning its mask, and both are sacrificed as a result of this love. Thus, when Hamlet and *Maud*'s narrator build a selfhood around their relationship with women, they ironically construct a self around the influence of powerless pawns. In doing so, they shift their discourse and persona in relation to their understanding of these women and blame them for their madness while not really understanding the relationship between the two. As the speakers are filters for the madness of an age, the women in their lives are filters for the madness of both age and speaker.

For instance, as I noted in a previous chapter, the narrator of *Maud* begins to embrace the moral madness of civil war when he hears his love "Singing of men that in battle array" are "Ready in heart and ready in hand" to "March with banner and bugle and fife / To the death, for their native land" (I.169-72). It is the fusion of her jingoism and her beauty that leads him down the path to ruin. He tells us that she, "in the light of her youth and her grace, / Singing of Death, and of Honor that cannot die" makes him " weep for a time so sordid and mean" and for himself: "so languid and base" (I.176-79) and later spurs his call to arms. Significantly, although this "beautiful voice" initially troubles his mind: "With a joy in which" he "cannot rejoice" and a "glory" he "shall not find" (I.180-83), when "the fires of hell and hate" break out over his corrupt "Eden" and "a million bloodthirsty bellowing echoes" break "from the red-ribb'd hollow behind the wood" he easily embraces "the Christless code" of honor through violence (II.7-27). This passage is significant because it shows that in his rage he associates Christ with a lack of honor and old testament justice with the bloodthirsty demands of personal vengeance. After he answers the call to bloodthirsty vengeance and recalls the scene of the murder, he links his former actions to bestial human nature and calls out:

> Arise, my God, and strike, for we hold Thee just,
> Strike dead the whole weak race of venomous worms,
> That sting each other here in the dust;
> We are not worthy to live. (II.45-48)

Clearly he expects the same old testament God whose sense of justice previously led him to murder to destroy humanity. Would God unfairly destroy us for possessing the impulses inspired by a sense of divine justice? Clearly the narrator expects his God to do just that. This God, although sometimes understood to be "an unseen hand at a game" (I.127), is clearly present at the site of bloody and vengeful murder. Moreover, like Hamlet, who also associates Heaven with strife and murder and plays God when embracing them, the narrator of *Maud* takes on the role he associates with God when, after the murder of Maud's brother, he stands at the seashore. At this point in the text, he is struck by how "a lovely shell, / Small and pure as a pearl," near his foot is "Frail, but a work divine" and "Made so fairily well / With delicate spire and whorl" a "miracle of design!" (II.49-56). Compare his description of the shell to Hamlet's description of humanity:

> What a piece of work is a man! how noble in reason!
> how infinite in faculty! in form and moving how
> express and admirable! in action how like an angel!
> in apprehension how like a god! the beauty of the
> world! the paragon of animals! (2.2.297-301).

62

Just as Hamlet sees humanity, in all its divine effects, as a mere "quintessence of dust" (2.2.302), the narrator of *Maud* sees the shell as mirroring humanity's spiritually stranded state:

> The tiny cell is forlorn,
> Void of the little living will
> That made it stir on the shore.
> Did he stand at the diamond door
> Of his house in a rainbow frill?
> Did he push, when he was uncurl'd,
> A golden foot or a fairy horn
> Thro' his dim water-world? (*Maud* II.61-68).

Significantly, Tennyson's hero then responds to it as he imagines God responds to us. Initially he had asked himself: "Why am I sitting here so stunn'd and still, / Plucking the harmless wild-flower on the hill" as "there rises ever a passionate cry / From underneath in the darkening land" that smolders with "The fires of Hell and of Hate" (II.2-10). However, he all too quickly moves from questioning his arbitrary cruelty to noting how easily he can crush the miraculous shell into dust, describing it as: "Slight, to he crush'd with a tap / Of my finger-nail on the sand" (II.69-70).

Furthermore, after the narrator murders Maud's brother and is haunted by her ghost, he all too easily embraces the joy and glory of jingoism that he once saw as beyond his reach. Now he imagines meadows, rivulets, light, and shadows dancing to her battle song (II.180-83), and he feels himself in harmony with such forces. When he hears her song again, he dreams of it as accompanied by the "sudden passionate cry" that heralds death, and the "sullen thunder" that "shakes the city" (II.189-90), yet he still hopes that Maud's "happy spirit" will take him to join her in "the realms of light and song" (II.221-28). At last she does, and when love spices "his banquet with the dust of death" (I.64) the "old hysterical mock disease" (III.33) of the speaker's hope for justice gives way to the promise of Mars: a promise that Britain's careless God will no longer be the "soul millionaire" of corruption and Peace's herds will not continue to grossly multiply (III.22-25). Such is akin to the moral madness that increasingly infects Hamlet and surfaces in response to how he perceives Ophelia and his mother. Hamlet increasingly embraces gratuitous murder, and the narrator of *Maud* increasingly embraces murder through jingoism. Hamlet, like his stepfather, is led to murder by self-interest, and the narrator of *Maud* is led to fight for the society whose chief representative is the old grey wolf. In doing so, both embrace the civil war that consumed the women, and the society, around them: a civil war they once faulted as the tool of God and Providence and now as heartily embrace as such. With love and spiritual faithlessness as the catalyst, both men "repell'd . . . Fell into a sadness . . .Thence to a watch, thence into a weakness, / Thence to a lightness, and, by this declension, into the madness wherein" they raved (*Hamlet* 2.2.146-50).

In the work of both Tennyson and Shakespeare, the earth is a fallen Eden full of screams and madness in which gross appetites, bestial oblivion, and consumption are given free reign. We have discussed the fact that Hamlet sees the world as "weary, stale, flat and unprofitable" and calls it "an unweeded garden" possessed by "things rank and gross in nature" because he associates his mother's love with bestial appetite (1.2.133-37). Ever comparing his father to his uncle, he simply cannot endure the fact that she could "on this fair mountain leave to feed, / And batten on this moor" (3.4.66-67). Love then, is a diseased appetite which feeds either on oneself or on another. Moreover, this is but one example of how nature and animal imagery are used throughout the play to destabilize the human presence on the great chain of being and prove that we are more beast then angel– that we aspire to dust rather than to the heavens. Indeed, one might say that the entire play is built around the central theme of things rank and gross in nature consuming one another and themselves. For example, the ghost calls Claudius an "adulterate beast" (1.5.42) for bedding the seemingly virtuous Queen, and Hamlet echoes these sentiments, yet, as his madness develops, he also uses bestial imagery to refer both to the action that he feels himself lacking and to the stasis he is ashamed of.

Hamlet clearly admires "rugged Pyrrhus," who, like a "Hyrcanian beast . . . Black as his purpose" and smear'd "With blood of fathers, mothers, daughters, sons" sought Priam "With eyes like carbuncles" (2.2.435-50). However, he describes his own lack of bloody action in similarly bestial terms. After he meets with the army of

Fortinbras, he expresses shame for his lack of action, this time describing lethergy as bestial and asking: "What is a man, / If his chief good and market of his time / Be but to sleep and feed? a beast, no more" and attributing the unused "large discourse" to both "Bestial oblivion" and cowardly "thinking too precisely on th' event" (4.4.33-50).

In Act four, Hamlet tells Rosencrantz and Guildenstern that the King keeps such officers as themselves "Like an apple, in / the corner of his jaw, first mouth'd, to be last swallow'd" (4.2.16-18). Thus, when Hamlet praises Horatio's stoicism and Horatio accuses him of flattery, Hamlet's reply: "No, let the candied tongue lick absurd pomp" (3.2.55), perhaps refers to Polonius, Rosencrantz, and Guildenstern. When he has Rosencrantz and Guildenstern executed for this flaw, showing a lack of reason, compassion, and judgement, he justifies their death in terms of the law of the jungle, for "'Tis dangerous when the baser nature comes / Between the pass and fell incensed points / Of mighty opposites" (5.2.60-62). In other words, they who would eat, fatter game have eaten. Hamlet's ultimate judgment is that humanity, however "noble in reason" and "infinite in faculty"– however angelic in action and "in apprehension . . . like a god!"– is but "the paragon of animals" and, to him, a "quintessence of dust" (2.2.297-302).

Hamlet is not the only speaker who describes humanity in such terms. For example, Laertes associates Hamlet's interest in Ophelia with destructive appetite, warning her that "the trifling of his favour" is but "a fashion and a toy in blood" that destroys what it consumes and makes her "A violet in the youth of primy nature," but "The perfume and suppliance of a minute" (1.3.5-9). Moreover, in Act 3, Guildenstern speaks to the King and calls it a holy enterprise to "keep those many bodies safe / That live and feed upon your majesty" (3.3.9-10). In act 4, Claudius tells Laertes that his love for Gertrude restrains him from punishing Hamlet for Polonius' murder, and that their love, like a "foul disease," is thus allowed to "feed / Even on the pith of life" (4.2.19-23). Taken as a whole, these images reveal a play built around the central image of a jungle– a paradoxically Darwinian world of nature red in tooth and claw in which human beings are animals, eating one another as they move further from the realm of angels and closer to that of dust. This central image reaches its ironic conclusion in Hamlet's discussion of the pointlessness of the laws of the jungle. Hamlet sees the worm as an "emperor" in its diet, for "we fat all creatures else to fat us" and "we fat ourselves for maggots," making a "fat king" and a "lean beggar" but "variable service" and "two dishes" atop "one table"(4.3.20-23). Moreover, the great Alexander, "returneth into dust," may be used to "stop a beer-barrel," and "Imperious Caesar, dead and turn'd to clay, / Might stop a hole to keep the wind away" (5.1.195-200), for, in a corrupt and fallen Eden, the weak are but food for the strong and ambitious, and the fattest of beasts are but the fools of nature.

Maud, like *Hamlet,* is full of images of consumption and nature red in tooth and claw. At his most influential, Maud's brother is an "oil'd and curl'd Assyrian bull" (I.233) who, inspired by a "finer politic sense," would gladly auction his sister's virtue for a vote (I.236). However, he soon degenerates into a mere "lump of Earth," (I.537) clogged and drowning in "the mud-honey of town"[9] (I.540-541). The hollow near the hall is red-lipped (I.2) after having swallowed the speaker's father: the victim whose ruin "gorged" the old gray wolf (I.20). In response, the speaker fears that Maud's beauty will likewise gorge itself on his innocence and make him "a lion claspt by a passion-flower" (I.489-996). The general population consists of serpentine fools who are guilty of "hissing in war" on their own hearthstones (I.24), "long-neck'd geese" who "are ever hissing dispraise / Because their natures are little" (I.153-54), and men who walk with their heads "in a cloud of poisonous flies" (I.150-55). Peace lords over a bestial orgy, and in his fear of being consumed by Maud's beauty the speaker imagines the beach as being consumed by the ocean (I.98-99).

Obsessed with the possibility of Maud's scorning him for another, the speaker's "morbid hate and horror" increase until he sees his hopelessness as "a morbid eating lichen fixt / On a heart half-turn'd to stone" (I.264-67). In sanity or madness, he cannot escape the fear that "a lord, a captain, a padded shape, / A bought commission, a waxen face, / A rabbit mouth that is ever agape" will consume her affection, leaving him "splenetic, personal, base, / A wounded thing with a rancorous cry" at war with himself and "a wretched race" and "Sick, sick" to the very "heart of life" (I.360-65). Love itself is at war with life; indeed, it is seen as consuming life, for "sullen-seeming Death may give / More life to Love than is or ever was / In our low world" and "Love, like men in drinking songs, spices "his fair banquet with the dust of death" (I.643-54).

Like Hamlet, the narrator of *Maud* maintains that humanity, the paragon of animals, aspires to less than "lesser" beasts, noting:

> A monstrous eft[10] was of old the Lord and Master of Earth,
> For him did his high sun flame, and his river billowing ran,
> And he felt himself in his force to be Nature's crowning race.
> As nine months go to the shaping an infant ripe for his birth,
> So many a million of ages have gone to the making of man:
> He now is first, but is he the last? is he not too base? (*Maud* I.132-37).

Thus, he, like Hamlet, has "An eye well-practiced in nature" and, consequently, "a spirit bounded and poor" (*Maud* I.138-39). Expressing the bleak state of humanity through the scientific landscape of their authors' ages, Hamlet sees the bestial nature of humanity as evidence of a disordered Great Chain of Being, while the narrator of *Maud* sees humanity's bestial nature in terms of the bleak evolutionary prophecies of Werner[11] and Lyell. In both cases, the destabilization of the human presence is seen as a sign of God's indifference and the absurdity of Providence. Hence, as Denmark is a rank garden in which beasts consume one another and themselves, England is a jungle in which "the spirit of murder" eats away at "the very means of life" (I.40).

As I noted in a previous chapter, Tennyson, referring to *Maud*, told his son: "The peculiarity of this poem is that the different phases of passion in one person take the place of different characters" (qtd. in H. Tennyson 1: 396). This use of antiphonal voice passages does much to intensify the relationship between Shakespeare's drama and Tennyson's monodrama. One possibility that has not been explored critically is that of Tennyson's narrator actually giving a voice to specific characters from the prior work. Clearly, the narrator of *Maud* often speaks with Hamlet's voice and, as does Hamlet himself, with the voices of Horatio and Laertes.

For example, both Hamlet and the speaker of *Maud* voice an obsession with death and suicide: each questions why he was, and wishes he had not been, born. The death of his father and hasty remarriage of his mother lead Hamlet to wish that his "too sallied flesh would melt, / Thaw, and resolve itself into a dew" (1.2.129-30). As dissolution is impossible, he wishes that suicide were not a sacrilege, continuing: "Or that the Everlasting had not fix'd / His canon 'gainst self- slaughter!" (1.2.129-32). After his father's ghost tells him to avenge his murder, Hamlet notes: "The time is out of joint– O cursed spite, / That ever I was born to set it right!" (1.5.188-190). When Polonius says he is going to take his leave of Hamlet in the fishmonger scene, Hamlet responds: "You cannot take from me any thing that I will not / more willingly part withal– except my life, except my life / except my life" (2.2.212-14). Moreover, in the "what a rogue and peasant slave am I" soliloquy (2.2.530-85), he once again questions whether it would be more noble to live and endure the lashes of fortune or commit suicide and thus oppose its brutality. Hamlet later arrives at the conclusion that to die is simply to sleep, thus to put an end to the suffering we inherit upon our birth and its ascent through fickle fortune's fancy. However, as we do not know "what dreams may come" after death, we cowardly choose to endure instead the "calamity" of our "mortal coil" (3.1.65-68). Thus, it is cowardice and not duty that leads us to endure "the whips and scorns of time," the chains of oppression, the scorn of the proud, the "pangs" of unrequited love, and the abuses of law and politics that vex our patience and make us "grunt and sweat" our way though a "weary life" (3.1.69-76). Hamlet, like the speaker of *Maud,* believes that the "pale cast of thought" often sickens "the power of resolution," not only in relation to suicide but in relation to all action (3.1.83-84), yet his response to civil war is to frequently mourn the occasion of his birth.

Likewise, as I noted previously, the death of his father and loss of his mother lead Tennyson's speaker to cry out: "For there in the ghastly pit long since a body was found, / His who had given me life–O father! O God! was it well?" (I.6), referring not only to his father's death but to his own birth as well. He rages that he too may "passively take the print / Of the golden age" for he has "neither hope nor trust" and expects merely to "Cheat and be cheated, and die" for humanity is but "ashes and dust" (I.29-32). The thought that he is "raging alone" as his father "raged in his mood" leads him to question if he too must "creep to the hollow" and "dash" himself "down and die" in order to escape brooding "On a horror of shattered limbs and a wretched swindler's lie" (I.53-56). As I also suggested in a previous chapter, such thoughts of suicide evolve into an obsession with sacrificing himself to Maud. The speaker affirms that his "clamorous heart" will voice his love for her "or die" (I.567-70) and the thoughts of her "death-white curtain drawn" lead him to shudder and imagine "like a fool of the sleep of death" (I.525-26). Shudders of fear soon give way to shudders of expectation, for "sullen-seeming Death may give / More life to Love than is or ever was / In our low world" (I.644-46). When Maud is finally made his by a "long loving kiss," this union leads him to the realization that "The dusky strand of Death interwoven here / With dear Love's tie, makes Love himself more dear" (I.656-59). After her death he addresses his own "poor heart of stone" and tells it to have courage, for "She is but dead, and the time is at hand / When thou shalt more than die" (II.132-40), and when her phantom rises one last time and flies "Far into the North, and battle, and seas of death" (III.37), he scorns the peace that he "deemed no peace" and offers himself up to be "crush'd in the clash of jarring claims" (III.44) and consumed by the "deathful-grinning mouths" of war (III.52).

Like Hamlet, Tennyson's narrator views suicide as an appropriate reaction to civil war. The difference between their views lies the fact that Tennyson's narrator is better able to rationalize away the moral implications of suicide by giving suicide a different name. Tennyson's character does not concern himself with the damnation he buys by courting his death because he believes that he is offering himself up as a sacrifice to love's "perfumed altar flame" (I.621) or to "the purpose of God" (III.359). Hamlet has to consider the fact that he, as the rightful ruler of Denmark, is God's chief political representative on Earth. Hence, he has not the option, morally, of doing away with his own life. Shakespeare's Lear is a fine example of what becomes of those who make such a mistake. For Tennyson's hero, the issue of morality is, at least in the hero's mind, irrelevant. If anything, he is likely to view

69

dying for love and for England as a moral victory, as answering the call of Maud's battle song, regardless of the means through which the death is achieved. Hamlet has no such rationale.

It is hard to imagine two men more opposite in nature than the emotional Hamlet and the rational Horatio, yet together they provide two sections of the fragmented self Tennyson will brilliantly bring to life in the antiphonal voices of *Maud*'s narrator. In Shakespeare's drama, we meet Horatio before Hamlet, and when Horatio shows up and Bernardo asks him: "What, is Horatio there?" (1.1.18), Horatio responds: "A piece of him" (1.1.19). Horatio is a stoic, and when he says that only a piece of him is there, this perhaps reflects the absence of the emotive part of human nature which he suppresses, the part that is nursed to full bloom in Hamlet, who views everything through the lens of his emotions. Thus, Horatio and Hamlet remain, in effect, fragments of a whole. Horatio's position as a fragment of Hamlet is made clear the first time we see them together. When first they meet, Hamlet notes: "I am glad to see you well / Horatio,--or I do forget myself" and, in response to Horatio's fond description of himself as Hamlet's "poor servant ever," he responds: "Sir, my good friend; I'll change that name with you (1.2.159-163). This mirroring is given another, even more poignant, layer as Hamlet's discussion of the funeral/wedding dichotomy mirrors the dichotomy of Horatio and himself. Here we find two sides of the same coin: just as "the funeral baked meats" do "coldly furnish forth the marriage tables" (I.180-81), Horatio's presence makes more evident the spiritual dissolution of Hamlet, who is already mad with grief and who already sees God and Fate in terms of strife and destruction.

Consider the words and actions of Hamlet and Horatio in the graveyard scene, a scene extremely important in how clearly it reveals their opposing reactions to civil war and a disordered universe. In a sense, the 2nd clown's assertion that "the / gallows is built stronger than the church" (5.1.45) voices the germ of Hamlet's madness. When Hamlet hears the clown sing while digging graves he asks Horatio: "Has this fellow no feeling of his business? a' sings in grave-making?" (5.2.64) and Horatio, as usual, responds without letting his emotions color his perception, noting that "Custom hath made it in him a property of easiness" (5.2.65). When Hamlet finally gets around to asking the clown whose grave it is, and challenging him with: "I think it be thine indeed, for thou liest in't" (5.1.114) the clown replies: "You lie out on't, sir, and therefore 'tis not yours; / for my part, I do not lie in't, and yet it is mine" (5.1.115-16). This exchange is particularly poignant and symbolic. The grave is indeed that of both Hamlet and the clown, and, in a sense, that of Denmark as well. Although it is intended for Ophelia, her suicide carves as fitting a headstone for the Denmark that was extinguished in scheming, self-interest, ambition, and civil war. Moreover, it serves as a marker of the spiritual death of both Hamlet, who sees death as an agent of nature red in tooth and claw, and the clown, who sees it as proof of the fact that death is mightier than the church. Thus, Hamlet speaks an ironic truth when he tells Horatio that "the age is grown so picked that the toe of the / peasant comes so near the heel of the courtier" (5.1.130-31).

In order to escape the injustice of this age, Hamlet longs for the stoicism that distinguishes him from Horatio, for as suicide is not an option for him, he seeks to escape the horror of civil war by dissolving himself in the defining features of his foils. Rather than himself: "Passions slave" (3.2.67) and an instrument for "fortune's finger to play on" (3.2.65), Hamlet would be a Horatio, who can accept fortune's blows without suffering and calamity. Unfortunately, Hamlet's disgust with humanity so colors his perception that he is incapable of maintaining such a rational and impersonal stance and is led instead to fragmentation. For example, in his description of dead Yorick, we see Hamlet stepping outside of himself to view the mad, disillusioned, chop-fallen thing he has become. Holding the skull, he superficially addresses himself to the rational Horatio, yet he may also be speaking of, and perhaps to, the part of himself that is incapable of Horatio's stoicism. Superficially addressing Horatio, Hamlet ponders how Yorick, a fellow "of infinite jest" who once carried him on his back, could have lost the "gibes . . . gambols . . . songs" and "flashes of merriment that were wont to set the table on a roar" and become "quite chop-fall'n" (5.1.72-79). Is it not Hamlet himself who has cast off all "gibes . . . gambols . . . songs" and "flashes of merriment" (5.1.76-77)? Is it not he who has lost the ability to laugh, and to carry the burden of life (5.1.73-81)? When Hamlet recognizes his own madness, he often does so from the vantage point of Horatio, the man who has no use for "wild and whirling words" (1.5.133) and sees the ghost of King Hamlet as "a mote" to "trouble the mind's eye" (1.1.112). Because he is incapable of the total stoicism he covets, his language remains marked by hyperbole and his "mind's eye" remains jaundiced, yet he is at least momentarily rational enough to be self-aware, a trait he lacks shamefully throughout most of the drama. Thus, to a slight degree, Hamlet will occasionally adopt the rational stance of his foil. However, instead of the stoicism he seeks, it leads him to back to the futility of his madness: a spiritual and moral sickness lodged, with the ever present image of his mother's bed, in his "mind's eye" (1.2.183-85).

Hamlet and Horatio's relationship as foils, or "pieces" of one another, is highlighted once more in the closing scene of the play, for in this most tragic conclusion they seem to actually switch roles. The mirror has been turned upside down, but its two faces retain their relationship to one another. When Horatio sees that Hamlet is dying, his response is that of Hamlet himself, as he considers suicide and cries out: "I am more an antique Roman than a Dane. / Here's yet some liquor left" (5.2.323). Hamlet, who had turned his back on God and Providence long ago, responds with Horatio's voice, noting that "By Heaven" (5.2.325) he will prevent him, affirming that he now sees Heaven as associated with justice, the position of Horatio with which the play opened. By Heaven, he asks Horatio to "Absent thee from felicity awhile, / And in this harsh world draw thy breath in pain / To tell my story" (5.2.329-31). Whereas Hamlet once praised Horatio for his ability to suffer fortune's arrows stoically, he must now ask that same friend to put aside his emotions and be rational. In response, Horatio closes the play with his own words, revealing emotion as if by accident and faith through emphasis, noting: "Now cracks a noble heart. Good night sweet prince: / And flights of angels sing thee to thy rest!" (5.2.341-42).

Tennyson quite brilliantly gives life to Horatio, Hamlet, and Laertes in the divided narrator of *Maud*'s antiphonal voice passages. For example, consider the opening section of the monodrama. Just as *Hamlet* opens with "a piece" of Horatio, *Maud* opens with a piece or fragment of its divided narrator: not the rational, more stoic persona, but the raging mad persona who, as we will see, speaks with the voice of Laertes. *Maud* opens, with "I hate" (I.1) and continues through the dappling and silent horror of blood to the pathetic reading of hate and bloodlust into the surrounding landscape. Thus, at the onset of the drama, it is clear that the speaker is already mad with grief and rage. However, following closely on the heels of this vitriolic outburst, there is a shift in tone and language as the stoical side of the speaker's persona takes over, asking: "Did he fling himself down? who knows? For a vast speculation had fail'd" (I.19). The voice we find here is the reasonable and unemotional voice of one who tries to rationally come to terms with the cause of his father's death, rather than obsessing over their emotional repercussions. In effect, this is the voice of a second generation Horatio. Its presence is particularly noticeable when compared to the aforementioned raging and the consonance and hurried effect of the voice that immediately follows it: "And ever he mutter'd and madden'd and ever wann'd with despair" (I.9). Here we see the speaker's emotive and rash persona once again taking control, which it does completely by the next line as the hero pathetically reads his emotions into nature: "And out he walked when the wind like a broken worldling wailed, / And the flying gold of the woodlands drove through the air" (I.11-12). Thus, we see that while *Hamlet* opens with the would-be piece of Hamlet known as Horatio, *Maud* opens with a disconnected dialogue in which the pieces of the speaker address one another. These alternating voices, or "pieces" continue to war with one another throughout the monodrama, giving life to Shakespeare's famous opposites, and proving that the man caught in the middle is indeed "mad north-north-west" (*Hamlet* 2.2.367).

Hamlet's recognition of the madness and spiritual malaise that lurk in his mind's eye is brought to life in the rational "piece" of Tennyson's fragmented persona, a piece which, like the clear-minded part of Hamlet, occasionally surfaces to comment on the imbalanced state of its other half, or, in this case, third. Just as Hamlet longs for the stoicism of Horatio and occasionally speaks with Horatio's voice, so does the second generation Hamlet: the narrator of *Maud*. Hamlet shares his inability to escape the vision of his dead father, or, to use Horatio's words, "mote" lodged in his mind's eye, and Tennyson's speaker comments on how his mind, "when fraught with a passion so intense / One would think that it well / Might drown all life in the eye," will "by being so overwrought" suddenly "strike on a sharper sense / For a shell, or a flower, little things / Which else would have been past by!" (II.106-113). Just as Hamlet is occasionally aware of his madness, a madness that stems from his fixation with his father's murder, his lady's Janus-like beauty, and his mother's sexuality, the narrator of *Maud* chastises himself for "raging alone" as his father "raged in his mood" and brooding "On a horror of shatter'd limbs and a wretched swindler's lie" (I.53-56). The sight of Maud's "hard mechanical ghost" leads him to see himself as "a shipwreck'd man on a coast" who is plagued with a "disease" or "a lying trick of the brain"(II.37) and a "juggle born of the brain" (II.79-90), which gives way to "a nameless fear"(II.92).

His madness eats away at him like "a morbid lichen fixt / On a heart half turned to stone" (I.267-68) and, desiring to escape it, he, like Hamlet, longs for the faith and stoical position of an alter ego. It may be said that the Hamlet in him longs to be a Horatio, even as his hyperbolic and pathetic speech make evident the futility of this desire. He too longs for "a philosopher's life in the quiet woodland ways," in which, if he "cannot be gay," a "passionless peace" may be his "lot" (I.150-51) and affirms, "Long have I sigh'd for a calm / God grant I may find it at last" (I.77). However, his references to God, like those of Hamlet, are but lip service, offered by the part of him that wants to believe in justice to the part of him that rejects it. This is particularly evident in the way he attempts to convince himself that one need not mourn if "the drift of the Maker is dark" (I.143), "weep if a Poland fall," or "shriek if a Hungary fail," for "He that made" the world "will guide" it (I.143-49). Part of him is trying to be stoical, yet another, more prominent, part of him, like that of Hamlet, links God to destruction. Even when he tries to don the girdle of faith, part of him can't help but see this girdle as one that oppresses and annihilates as it enfolds. Just as Hamlet proves himself incapable of Horatio's stoical reaction to injustice, the narrator of

Maud proves he cannot be indifferent to the abuses of an age in which "the long-neck'd geese of the world" and "the clamour of liars belied in the hubbub of lies" refuses to leave him in peace (I.152-54). Although Hamlet and his Victorian counterpart turn to stoicism to escape the madness of an ambitious, malign society and the cruel, false promise of love, each finds himself incapable of fully embracing what he seeks.

Hamlet's inability to remain either north or north-west hurries him, over the mid point, to and from raging passion and stoicism. Hence, just as part of Hamlet longs to adopt the defining feature of Horatio, another part of him longs to adopt the defining characteristic of Laertes and Fortinbras. Moreover, just as Hamlet occasionally adopts some of Horatio's sensibility and speaks somewhat with Horatio's rational voice, he also dons the fiery passions of Laertes and voices his bloodlust and jingoism. Hamlet is indeed "mad north-north-west" (2.2.367), and when he swings from north to west, he vacillates between the two extreme personas he prefers to his own torturous indecision. Conflicted, tormented, and incapable of stoicism, Hamlet will turn to, and occasionally embrace, the heedless passion of Laertes: his other mirror image, or "piece."

Where Hamlet's erratic contemplation often makes it impossible for him to trade reflection for action, Laertes seems incapable of reflection and satisfied to let consuming passions lead him frantically from rash deed to rash deed. Indeed, Laertes is every bit as rash as Horatio is mild. When he returns from exile after his father's death, Laertes throws Hamlet's flaws into the foreground when he gathers a mob to storm the castle and voices sentiments that rightfully belong to Hamlet, in a fiery language Hamlet uses only at his most irrational:

> That drop of blood that's calm proclaims me bastard,
> Cries cuckold to my father, brands the harlot
> Even here between the chaste unsmirched brow
> Of my true mother. (4.5.116-119)

Like Hamlet when corrupted by the lust for personal vengeance and the narrator of *Maud* when corrupted by the false promise of Mars, Laertes embraces the lawlessness and brutality of civil war. He will "be revenged / Most thoroughly" for the loss of his father (4.5.134-35) by cutting Hamlet's throat in a church, and the tears he would shed at the loss of his sister will not be allowed to silence the "speech of fire, that fain would blaze" (4.7.190-91). Hamlet, too, wishes to set ablaze his speech. Indeed, he so wishes to voice his sense of injustice and foul play that, against his will, his conversations with his mother and Ophelia bubble over with defensive spite. Thus, when Hamlet speaks with Laertes' voice and vehemence, he loses the moral legitimacy Laertes maintains because his fiery words are directed primarily at his much maligned mother and his perplexed lady. With equally unfortunate consequences, he seeks to set ablaze the physical, emasculated part of himself that languishes in contemplation. Just like the narrator of *Maud*, Hamlet wants to achieve signification through action and, as the play progresses, his actions become increasingly corrupt, cruel, self-interested, and self-righteous.

Just as the relationship between Hamlet and Horatio is represented symbolically in the wedding/funeral dichotomy and in Hamlet's comment that he will change names with Horatio, his relationship with his other would-be self, Laertes, is depicted symbolically in the graveyard scene. Laertes, at his sister's burial, leaps into her grave to catch her once more in his arms, visually representing the death of the part of him that held love as a refuge. In response to Laertes' tortured outburst, Hamlet leaps into the grave with him and, speaking with Laertes' voice, expresses Laertes' inability to control his anger: " . . . though I am not splenitive and rash, / Yet have I something in me dangerous, / Which let thy wisdom fear" (5.1.246-48). He then offers the following, extremely selfish, challenge: "I loved Ophelia: forty thousand brothers / Could not, with all their quantity of love, / Make up my sum" (5.1.255-57). Narcissistically suggesting that Laertes came to the graveyard to "outface" him "with leaping in her grave" (5.1.264), he responds: "I'll rant as well as thou" (5.1.269). Hamlet, who at this point has no reason to suspect that Laertes is incensed against him, shows no respect for a brother's loss and instead seeks to war over who loved Ophelia most. Such is quite ironic, given the fact that when she was alive he treated her with unwarranted and merciless cruelty. Whereas previously Hamlet was playing mad as his madness took him over, he now tries to play the mourner, and, again the role dissolves in moral madness. When Hamlet asks Laertes "What is the reason that you use me thus?" (5.1.275), he seems quite selfishly indifferent to the righteous anger of one who lost a father and a sister to his influence. He then notes: "it is no matter. / Let Hercules himself do what he may, / The cat will mew and dog will have his day" (5.1.276-78), implying that no sign of strength or heroism can effect the outbursts of lower creatures and not realizing he, more so than Laertes, has been reduced to the unreasoning, amoral passions housed one link lower on the chain of being.

The death of Ophelia leads Hamlet to adopt the aggression and moral malaise associated with Laertes because Hamlet seeks desperately to reject the powerlessness Laertes marks in him by comparison, and this self-consuming empowerment resurfaces in Tennyson's drama with the death of Maud's brother. Tennyson's speaker is enraged because Maud's brother "fiercely" gives him "the lie" that their love cannot be. This threatens the part of the speaker that, albeit begrudgingly, seeks Maud's love as a form of signification, just as Hamlet is threatened by Laertes' stronger signs of mourning and love for Ophelia. In response, the hero of *Maud* "with as fierce an anger spoke," and when the brother fought the verbal lashing with physical aggression, the brother "Struck for himself an evil stroke" and "Wrought for his house an irredeemable woe," revising Laertes' physical assault of Hamlet (II.21-22). The physical mirroring of Hamlet and Laertes in the grave also resurfaces, as "front to front" Tennyson's hero stands with Maud's brother, and Hamlet's enraged assault on Leartes' love for his sister resurfaces as "a million horrible bellowing echoes" break "From the red-ribb'd hollow behind the wood" and lead the narrator to adopt "the Christless code, / That must have life for a blow"(II.9-27) Just as Hamlet tries to subvert Laertes' power and, in doing so, assaults both his rational and his irrational ideals, the Christless code that undoes Maud's brother undoes the possibility of the hero's sane existence, making the life undone "for a blow," in effect, his own (II.27).

The sight of Fortinbras' army marching against Poland "to gain a little patch of ground / That hath in it no profit but the name"(4.4.17-18) appears to Hamlet "the imposthume of much wealth and peace, / That inward breaks, and shows no cause without / Why the man dies" (4.4.27-29), yet this disease leads him to ponder the famous question repeated by Tennyson's Ulysses: "What is a man, / If his chief good and market of his time / Be but to sleep and feed? a beast, no more" (*Hamlet* 4.4.33-35). Evidence of Hamlet's increasing corruption is presented in the fact that in the wake of this sight he praises Fortinbras for being "a delicate and tender prince, / Whose spirit with divine ambition puff'd" exposes "what is mortal and unsure / To all that fortune, death, and danger dare, / Even for an egg-shell" (4.4.48-53). Thus, we see that Hamlet, who once equated justice with mourning the fall of every sparrow, finds so great an honor in heralding "The imminent death of twenty thousand men" simply to "find quarrel in a straw" that he is led to voice the pledge: "O, from this time forth, / My thoughts be bloody, or be nothing worth!" (4.4.60-66). Such makes apparent the fact that his values are becoming relative and more like those of his age, for he apparently doesn't recognize the irony in praising what God gave us AND the lofty cause of extinguishing such gifts in order to gain a useless piece of straw. Whereas he just described Fortinbras' actions as a sickness or disease produced by "much wealth and peace" (4.4.27), he now feels ashamed because he lacks such sickness.

Similarly, Maud's "chivalrous battle-song" leads Tennyson's hero to assert that "She would not do herself this great wrong, / To take a wanton dissolute boy / For a man and leader of men" (I.386-88). Then, addressing the God he only seems to recognize in conjunction with violence, the waylaid boy muses :

> Ah God, for a man with heart, head, hand,
> Like some of the simple great ones gone
> For ever and ever by,
> One still strong man in a blatant land,
> Whatever they call him, what care I,
> Aristocrat, democrat, autocrat—one
> Who can rule and dare not lie.
> And ah for a man to arise in me,
> That the man I am may cease to be! (I.389-97).

Like Hamlet, he cares not with what name and moral code the "still strong man" appears, so long as that man "can rule" and dares to avoid "the lie" of hypocritically raging under the surface yet not taking action (I.95-97). He, like Hamlet, equates justice with fighting for the ambition and pride he once railed against and, in doing so, imagines himself championing "the purpose of God and the doom assigned" (*Maud* III.59). Thus, a sense that "conscience does make cowards of us all" may lead both heroes to remember "the name of action," yet in the type of aggression they covet, what is "sicklied o'er" is not "the hue of resolution" but the pale cast of conscience (*Hamlet* 3.1.81-84).

The issue at hand, then, is whether or not the Laertes "piece" of Hamlet and his Victorian counterpart is worth the sacrifice it demands. Can it provide the listless whole with the ease from suffering sought, in vain, in Stoicism? Unable to restrain their passions and silently endure the whips and scorns of civil war, will Hamlet and Tennyson's hero be content, as Laertes and Fortinbras seem to be, at cracking the whip and scorning the consequences? When Hamlet silences the running dialogue in his mind and stops trying to "do the right thing" is ignorance really bliss? When the narrator of *Maud* unleashes his righteous anger against his lover and oppressor, does he find refuge in the Christless code of civil war?

Unleashing his Herculean passions on those around him doesn't seem to make Hamlet feel better, yet there is poignant incongruity in his reaction to having doing so. The murder of Polonius is a trifle: a game engendered by a sycophant's having lived long enough to be a fool, and that of his school chums is rationalized away as mere social Darwinism. Venting his fear and frustration on Gertrude has little effect on him, for the only direct response he shows to her murder is "Wretched Queen, adieu" (5.2.315), proving that she never climbed out of the incestuous bed she lay strewn across in her son's mind's eye. After Ophelia dies, Hamlet seems to feel no remorse for unfairly unleashing his frustration and spite on her. Instead, he uses shows of mourning her merely to out-do those of Laertes. Just as the death of Yorick leads him to step out of himself and, while superficially addressing Horatio, speak to the part of himself that wants to be like Horatio, the death of Ophelia leads him to don the rashness of Laertes and, while superficially raging at Laertes, direct his words toward the less aggressive "piece" of himself, defensively trying to convince it that it can "rant as well" as a grieving brother (5.1.270).

Similarly, the more Tennyson's hero tries to escape the shackles of his own madness and fear, the more tightly he finds himself bound by them. His longing for "nerves of motion as well as the nerves of pain" and desire to reject "the pit and the fear" (I.63-4) lead him to seek refuge in a hyacinth girl. Such is a refuge that dissolves like a mirage as the girl herself becomes the sharpest point in the trap, the bloodied rose gorged to full bloom under the shadow of the lily. In response, the part of him that tried to find himself in her tries to find himself in rejecting her and finds the experience equally unempowering.

For example, the scorning of her beauty hangs a terrifying phantom over him in bed, a vision from which the only clear path of escape leads to a sea boiling over with screams and terrors. Likewise, his self-defensive rejection of her pitying smile sends ghastly abominations streaming after him from the gleaming wood. Following him home in the middle of the day, thoughts of his own stony heart shadow him in hate and horror like the ruins of the afternoon. Indeed, the more he tries to convince himself that he can reject her, the more his attempt to do so makes apparent his sense of helplessness before her. In spite of the snub that followed his stammering before her in the village, his all too fleshy heart is "caught" by that "strong wine of love" it "swore to withstand" (I.268). In response, he turns his aggression toward Maud's brother, and the Christless blow he directs toward him resounds in the drop of a second victim and annihilates its own purpose. Thus, when Maud's ghost sends its victim off to fight in the Crimean war, it closes the last door on a man who rushed futilely, headlong, into the void and a soul whose only escape once laid in eternity.

Hamlet, too, rushes headlong into the void of insanity and embraces it with few apparent regrets. Significantly, the only abuse Hamlet seems to chastise himself for is his abuse of Laertes. Thus, can we help but be surprised by Hamlet's admission of remorse: "But I am very sorry, good Horatio, / That to Laertes I forgot myself" (5.2.75-76)? Why is Laertes singled out for consideration? There is nothing in the text to suggest that Laertes and Hamlet were particularly close. Indeed, Hamlet is indifferent to Laertes' departure at the beginning of the play, and Laertes seems to have little regard for Hamlet, whose love for Ophelia he sees merely as "trifling" and no more than the "perfume and suppliance of a minute" (1.3.5-9), so why is Laertes singled out for consideration? Hamlet mourns his ill treatment of Laertes because, although he feels threatened by Laertes' passions, he sub-consciously knows that disempowering Laertes will destroy the aggressive persona he desperately covets but cannot maintain. Subconsciously recognizing himself incapable of Laertes' total heedlessness, Hamlet becomes even more desperately protective of it. Such is quite similar to the way the narrator of *Maud* rushes off in desperation to fight in the Crimean war, courting his own destruction in spite of the fact that he subconsciously realizes the futility of embracing selfhood through soldierhood, as evident in his use of the word "doom." When Hamlet treats Laertes cruelly, he attacks the "piece" of himself that he would nurse to full bloom. Thus, he tells Horatio: "But, sure, the bravery of his grief did put me/ Into a towering passion," yet he regrets this passion because in "the image" of his desperate cause, he finds "The portraiture" of Laertes. (5.2.76-79).

Moreover, just as Hamlet and Horatio switch roles the last time they are together, so do Hamlet and Laertes. Laertes, seemingly for the first time, appears to be aware of his rash behavior and its moral implications and, after telling Osric: "I am justly kill'd with mine own treachery" (5.2.289), he admits to Hamlet: "Unbated and envenom'd: the foul practise / Hath turn'd itself on me" (5.2.299-300). Hamlet's response is to assault his Uncle and rage at him with Laertes' voice: "Here, thou incestuous, murderous, damned Dane, / Drink off this potion. Is thy union here? / Follow my mother" (5.2.307-09). Because he rages at an Uncle who he would have follow a still maligned mother into Hell, we see that Hamlet's north-west fragment , like that of Tennyson's hero, is no friend to the piece of him that reaches for the center.

A final degeneration into Herculean passion is represented in a Herculean swan song as the cacophony of civil war that trumpeted for Claudius and clashed for

Mammon blares for Hamlet and his Victorian counterpart. When Hamlet agreed not to go back to Wittenberg, and Claudius realized that he could keep the young prince under his thumb, the King boasted that "the great cannon to the clouds shall tell, / And the king's rouse the heavens all bruit again, / Re-speaking earthly thunder" as trumpets blared and cannons pounded. As "The kettle-drum and trumpet" once brayed Claudius' "triumph" over justice (1.4.10-12), Hamlet's verbal assault of his mother in the closet is a moral degeneration that "roars" and "thunders in the index" (3.4.53). Likewise, the "million horrible echoes" (II.124) that once roared over a bloodied heath and the pounding of Timor-Mammon's army that shook "a thousand thrones" (I.46) erupt again as Tennyson's hero joins the "clash of jarring claims" and adds his voice to the "battle cry" of a populace that, unified behind the banner of greed and avarice, dusts the cobwebs of Peace from the "cannon's throat" (III.27). Hamlet dies as drums sound the entrance of Fortinbras, and, as he is borne "like a soldier to the stage," the "soldier's music and the rite of war" sound as "loudly for him" (5.2.378-82) as they do at the last for the hero of *Maud*. When booms and blasts suffuse England and Denmark, the only satisfaction Hamlet and his Victorian counterpart can achieve from adopting a warlike persona is that found in the total annihilation of the alternate sides of their being. Once "The fires of Hell and of Hate" (*Maud* II.10), break from the rising sun, "the clash of jarring claims" bloodies the battlefield of selfhood and makes a martyr of contemplation (*Maud* III.44). When the cannons last boom, they sound for Leartes.

Thus, for Tennyson as well as for Shakespeare, the ultimate sacrifice was that of virtue. Through the genius of a perspicacious playwright and the mastery of a dramatic monologist, the tragedy of a man who sought to reconstruct himself, and the mirrors and catalysts at the heart of this foundation, were reborn three centuries later in the threadbare pastiche of a divided consciousness. Through the efforts of two of the world's most accomplished and talented writers, what unfolds before us is a tragedy of lofty idealism at war with "a wretched race" and with itself (*Maud* I.364). In both cases, the war is waged on the battlefield of "a wounded thing with a rancorous cry" (*Maud* I.363), set in a landscape diseased by civil war, and painted over the canvas of an age in which religious and scientific concerns falsified Divine will and the shadow of Eve blackened beauty with the visage of Janus. The critical hissing directed toward the so-called morbidity of Tennyson's "little *Hamlet,*" like that of the Puritans directed at Renaissance drama, was nothing more than the breathless gasp of those who, in the mirror of a timely and poignant work of art, found an imperfect human face staring back at them.

Thus, when we look with new eyes at the work Tennyson thought the finest accomplishment of his career, we find the genius of a man who drew from the well of England's greatest drama a tale of an ill-fated narcissist, washed it in the most vibrant purples of Romantic pathos, and glossed it over with the mysticism of nineteenth century England's most revolutionary painters. Such a melding of England's greatest artistry gave birth to an work so intricate in design and lofty in execution, and so honestly and unabashedly tragic, that Tennyson's peers were often aghast and outraged by its presentation of the sins of the age. When Tennyson sounded the trumpet for England, the most soul-wrenching of Tennysonian symphonies charmed countless scores of readers to the edge of the pool and dared them to peer into the precipice.

Chapter Four

An Annotated Bibliography of *Maud* Scholarship

While much nineteenth-century scholarship treats in detail the supposed Spasmodic qualities of Maud, much twentieth century scholarship labels Maud a Spasmodic work without offering the reasoning behind the label, seemingly taking for granted the monodrama's supposed Spasmodic heritage. This chapter, rather than noting each instance in which the term Spasmodic is used to refer to Tennyson's monodrama, explores themes central to the works in question. Thus, it treats the issue of Spasmodic heritage only when that issue is a focal point of the critical work being discussed.

Aaron, Jonathan. "The Idea of the Novelistic Form: A Study of Four Victorian
    'Verse-Novels' by Clough, Tennyson, and Browning." Diss. Yale, 1974.
Aaron examines Maud, *and three other poems, as verse novels. See Beetz: entry 4519.*

Albright, Daniel. *Tennyson: The Muses' Tug-of-War*. Virginia Victorian Studies 2.
    Charlottesville: UP of Virginia, 1986.
In his well written and fascinating chapter, "The Speaker of Maud *as Adonis," Albright traces in* Maud *his idea that at the heart of Tennyson's best work lies a tension between the sublime and the commonplace, a tension that surfaces in the monodrama through a hero who is ever in danger of slipping into the sublime and the mythical. The hero's love interest is described as a manifestation of his desire to create for himself the role of the mortal who worships a goddess from afar. Thus, when she alternately seems the Earthy coquette he, intolerant of ambiguity, is horrified by the contrast and its attendant spoiled sublimity. Hence, the goddess gives way to the wraith who haunts his dreams, and mythology remains a refuge from nothingness.*

"Alfred Tennyson." *Putnam's Monthly Magazine* (Oct. 1855): 382-92.
This review describes Maud *as having fused the emotion of Tennyson's early poems with the thought of his later poems and as a dramatic lyric that includes a passionate*

85

intensity unmatched in Tennyson's previous work. Refuting the critics who scorn the hero's morbidity, the reviewer claims that the hero's sensibility admirably delineates the moody, shrewd, subtle, sentimental, and philosophical youth of the age.

Armstrong, Isobel. "Tennyson in the 1850s: From Geology to Pathology, *In Memoriam* (1850) to *Maud* (1855)." *Victorian Poetry: Poetry, Poetics, and Politics.* New York: Routledge, 1993.
Armstrong suggests that In Memoriam, *rather than* Maud *is the exceptional text in the Tennyson canon, for the monodrama returns to Tennyson's early poetry of sensation and consciousness. She treats the shift between the two texts in terms of a movement from the geological subsurface in* In Memoriam *to the pathological excavation of the layered self in* Maud.

Assad, Thomas J. "Tennyson's 'Courage, Poor Heart of Stone.'" *Tulane Studies in English* 18 (1970): 73-80.
Assad explores the theme of the stony heart, expressed explicitly in the third section of Part II, as a central metaphor in the poem— one that evolves from the speaker's desire to remain immune to love by casting his heart in stone to an ambiguous fusion of pity and chastising directed toward the less defended heart with the call to courage in arms. In other words, the call to stone is both a call to a stupifying indifference and a chastisement of the heart for being stupidly alive.

"The Assembly of Extremes." *Crayon* 3 (Jan. 1856): 30-32.
The reviewer treats Maud *and Whitman's* Leaves of Grass *together, judging both morbid and deficient in form.*

A.Y. "Quarterly Review on Mr. Tennyson's *Maud*." *Macmillan's Magazine* 1 (Dec. 1859): 114-15.
The reviewer praises Maud *for its wholly dramatic presentation of Victorian social malaise and refutes the assertions of those who see the narrator's views as representing those of Tennyson himself.* Maud *is described as a long, sustained dramatic enterprise nearly equal in mastery to* Hamlet *and* King Lear, *and a more novel, striking experiment than any found in previous literature*

Aytoun, William Edmonstoune. "Macaulay." *Blackwood's Edinburgh Magazine* 80 (Sept. 1856): 665-80.
On page 365 of an essay on Macaulay, Aytoun begrudgingly praises the construction with which Maud's *plot, however poor and unworthy, is framed.*

---. Rev. of *Maud*, by Alfred Tennyson. *Blackwood's Edinburgh Magazine* 78 (Sept. 1855): 311-21. Rpt. in *Littell's Living Age* 47 (Oct. 6, 1855): 51-59.
In this famously caustic review, Aytoun describes Maud *as the morbid, unwholesome and wholly disagreeable product of a poet who mistreated his reading public by penning it. The reviewer sees it as neither poetry nor respectable verse but an ill-conceived and worse expressed pastiche of bombast.*

"Bailey and Tennyson." *Scottish Review* 3 (Oct. 1855): 347-57.
Beginning with the premise that Tennyson and Philip Bailey are not of the same

poetic school, the reviewer links Tennyson to Goethe at his weakest and suggests that the comparison often made between Tennyson and Shakespeare is merited only by a comparison of the Laureate's best work to the least accomplished of Shakespeare's works: the sonnets and "Venus and Adonis." Maud is described as a very weak enterprise, with the passage in which the hero notices the rings on Maud's slain brother's hand being the most absurd poetic passage ever penned. The reviewer's overall judgment is that Maud proves that Tennyson's poetic vein is nearly exhausted.

Basler, Roy. "Tennyson's *Maud.*" *Sex, Symbolism and Psychology in Literature.*
New Brunswick: Rutgers UP, 1948.
Basler provides a Freudian interpretation of Maud by describing the speaker's psychic struggle in terms of an Oedipal battle between Eros and Death. In the speaker's mind, sexuality is linked to natural law, and the subjective world of the speaker's own ego is linked to spiritual dignity. This explains the fact that he initially suppresses his love for Maud. Eros and Death are conjoined when Maud takes on the role of the speaker's conscience and leads him to sacrifice and atonement. Balser suggests that critics dismiss Maud because they resent its suggestion that all psychic phenomena is relative and the embracing of impossible ethical absolutes dooms us to barbarism. He also notes that the unfortunate, negative early reviews of it deflected Tennyson's natural bent toward psychological phenomena. According to Basler, Maud is a prime example of Tennyson's having anticipated Freud in his presentation of the narrator's early childhood trauma, and childhood identification of Maud with sexual love

---. "Tennyson the Psychologist." *SAQ* 43 (1944): 143-59.
Basler treats Maud as a study of psychic frustration: the struggle of self against an infantile conscience that links humanity and sexuality to brutal cruelty and pain. See "Tennyson's Maud." Sex, Symbolism and Psychology in Literature.

Literary History of England. Ed. Albert C. Baugh. London: Routledge, 1948.
On page 1368, Samuel Chew Links Maud to the Spasmodic closet dramas.

Bayne, Peter. "Tennyson and his Teachers." *Essays in Biography and Criticism.*
Boston, 1857. 50-145.
Bayne praises Tennyson's poetry, with the exclusion of Maud. See Beetz: entry 441

---. "The Two Versions of *Maud.*" *Literary World* [London] 18 Oct. 1878:
248-251. *Bayne describes Tennyson's revisions of Maud.*
See Beetz: entry 890.

Beasley, Violet Esther. *Alfred Lord Tennyson: Memory in Tennyson's Poetry.*
Diss. New York U, 1983. Ann Arbor: UMI, 1983. 8405752.
Beasley explores the influence of memory on Maud's speaker's madness and pathos.

Beesemyer, Irene. "'Black with the Void from which God Himself has Disappeared': Spatial Displacement in Tennyson's Maud. Tennyson Research Bulletin 7(2000): 174-190.
Beesemyer examines the central problem of Maud's hero as one of a systematized and irrevokable denial of signification through land affiliation or ownership.

Beetz, Kirk. Tennyson, A Bibliography, 1827-1982. Scarecrow Author Bibliographies 68. Metuchen: Scarecrow, 1984.
Maud entries are cross-referenced in the present bibliography.

Belcher, Margaret. "'Sane but Shattered': The Ending of Tennyson's Maud. Journal of the Australasian Universities Language and Literature Association: A Journal of Literary Criticism, Philology & Linguistics 50 (1978): 224-34.
Belcher explores Maud as ironic not only in its conclusion but from start to finish, and cites this undercurrent of irony as proof that Tennyson was indeed distanced from his speaker. Her examination of the poem's conclusion reveals what she sees as Tennyson's clear moral assertion: the "heart of fire" consumes itself.

Bennett, James. "Maud Part III: Maud's Battle Song." Victorian Poetry 18 (1980): 35-49.
By tracing the speaker's relationship with his love interest, and the selfhood he finds in that love interest, Bennett refutes the idea that Part III of Maud seems merely tacked on at the end, or is a digression from the love story at the heart of the poem. Bennett treats the jingoism in Part III in the context of the work as a whole, tracing through it the speaker's relationship with Maud, with God, and with his native land. Bennett notes that the narrator, in Parts I and II, alternates between seeing Maud as loving and warlike: qualities fighting for the surface in himself. In Part I, the loving Maud helps to relieve him of his violent impulses. In Part II, his aggressive nature resurfaces in the duel. In Part III, the two visions of both of them fuse. The aggressive warlike Maud sings the battle song favored by the gentle Maud, but the song is all that is left of her. Having her lead the way to battle represents, in his subconscious, forgiveness for slaying her brother and thus ending the reign of the gentle Maud and the gentle self. Thus, the spirit who points to Mars in Part III is a figment of his imagination, created by his conscience, in his madness, and the issue of jingoism is secondary to that of the speaker's love interest.

---. "The Historical Abuse of Literature: Tennyson's Maud: A Monodrama and the Crimean War." English Studies: A Journal of English Language and Literature 62 (1981): 34-45.
Bennett appropriately notes that historians and literary critics continue to equate simplistically Tennyson with the speaker of Maud. In response, he seeks to examine Tennyson's impression of the Crimean war, both personally and as presented through the eyes of his hero. In the course of such, in addition to highlighting the fact that Maud is a dramatic work and its sentiments those of a fictive persona, Bennett makes the interesting point that any attempt to explore Tennyson's personal reaction to the Crimean War is pure conjecture. He then notes that Tennyson's Francophobian reaction to the tyranny of Napoleonic France surfaced in several

poems, while he gave no such textualization to any anti-Russian and pro-Turkish sentiments he may have held. Moreover, he suggests that there is no evidence to support the possibility that the oversimplified reactions of his mad narrator are the sign of similarly extreme and one sided impressions on the poet's part. Bennett suggests that the poet's attitude toward Turkey is similarly complicated, for Tennyson cannot be said to have supported Turkish rule in Europe, and his hero's attitude toward Turkey is equally ambiguous. For example, while the hero denounces Nicholas, Maud's brother, hardly a likeable character, is labeled the Sultan on several occasions.

Bennett, W. C. *Anti-Maud: By a Poet of the People*. London, 1855.
A hilarious but scathing parody of Maud *that exaggerates the supposed "offenses" of the original work: its jingoism and its morbid portrait of avarice and Mammonism in Victorian England.*

Berglund, Lisa. "Faultily Faultless: The Structure of Tennyson's *Maud*." *Victorian Poetry* 27 (1989): 45-59.
Berglund argues that the monodrama does indeed have dramatic unity, and that to treat it as a mere collection of lyrics, or to read but excerpts of it, is to completely misread the poem and overlook the relationship between its central themes and its metrics. She treats the passages that are generally held up as faulty, such as "Go not happy day," and points out that such passages jar because they are so strikingly different from the manner in which the speaker usually expresses himself, and that the seeming inadequacy of his verbal framing reflects his inadequate understanding of the world around him. Berglund suggests that the narrator's language is set up as at odds with its content in order to illustrate the speaker's inability to lend meaning to the world around him through language, that his madness makes decoding that world impossible and his seemingly ill crafted passages reveal how very out of touch with that world he is, making the ending of the poem perversely comic.

"The Book Buyer." Review of *Maud*, by Alfred Tennyson. *Illustrated London News* 11 Aug. 1855: 183.
A brief review of Maud *mentioned on page 416 of Shannon's "Critical Reception."*

Bowden, Marjorie. *Tennyson in France*. Manchester: Manchester UP, 1930.
Bowden briefly outlines the critical reaction of the French to Tennyson's work, yet I found more interesting and useful a discussion of the French translation of Maud *that was penned by a man who was presumed mad. In a section of Tennyson's longer poems, Bowden describes the sole French translation of* Maud, *the work of an insane provincial doctor named Henri Fauvel. This translation was published in 1892 by Lemale at Havare. The translator describes the monodrama as the gloomiest of Tennyson's poems, yet a work that appeals to him in its accurate expression of the suffering of a heart embittered by the age yet longing for health. Bowden notes that the morbid despair of the hero is well translated, but the work as a whole suffers from numerous linguistic blunders on Fauvel's part. Nevertheless, it is interesting that Tennyson's portrait of madness generated the empathy of one*

who was presumed insane, so much that he undertook a translation he was barely equipped for.

Brimley, George. "Alfred Tennyson's Poems." *Cambridge Essays: Contributed
    by Members of the University.* London, 1855: 226-81. Rpt. in *Essays by the
    Late George Brimley.* Ed. William G. Clark. Cambridge, 1858. 1-103.
In the remarks on Maud *that elicited Tennyson's praise, Brimley answers the critics
who accuse Tennyson of morbidity. He begins by poignantly questioning whether,
through such reasoning, Shakespeare and Milton would not be equally morbid in
their presentation of tragic figures amidst bleak circumstances. He also suggests
that the speaker's madness flows from the same emotional well as his keen
sensibility, powerful emotions, and vivid imagination, and that madness is an
appropriate response, on the part of such a man, to such horrors and surroundings
as those he faces.*

Brinton, D.G. "The Beauties of *Maud.*" *Yale Literary Magazine* 22
    (Aug 1857):358-61.
Brinton likens Maud*'s detractors to a flock of sheep following one another to
unqualified disapprobation of the monodrama. He then praises the poem for
suggesting to the English mind the great moral lesson that life should be lived
earnestly and unselfishly. He says that Tennyson's narrator is equal to Goethe's
Werther in feeling but superior to him in intellect, and praises the narrator's shift
from cynicism to philanthropy.*

Brisman, Leslie. "*Maud*: The Feminine as the Crux of Influence." *Studies in
    Romanticism* 31.1 (Spring 1992): 21-43.
Brisman suggests that Maud *illustrates Michael Cooke's concept of gender typing
in literature, wherein masculine attributes are acquisitive and feminine attributes are
cumulative, the feminine being the "crux of value." The idealized Maud is,
according to Brisman, associated with cumulative delight, whereas the speaker
finally succumbs to masculine acquisitiveness by giving up thoughts of her to go to
war.*

Bristow, Joseph. "Nation, Class, and Gender: Tennyson's *Maud* and War."
    Genders 9 (1990): 93-111.
In this interesting textual and cultural analysis, Bristow explores Maud *as a work
that raises questions about masculinity and femininity in relation to politics and
commerce, in relation to class, and in relation to poetic genius. He treats such issue
as the association of nationalism with gender and the fact that, in Victorian England,
even patriotism was drawn along gender lines. Class politics led to an association
between pro-war sentiments, feudalism, and masculinity, while peace hawking
radicals were associated with industry, commerce, and femininity. The narrator of
the monodrama is featured as one who embraces both poles. His jingoism is aligned
with masculine, feudal nationalism, yet his fall into madness is seen as a feminized
rejection of that very system.*

Brooke, Stopford Augustus. *Tennyson : His Art and Relation to Modern Life.*
London, 1894.
In this very positive critique, Brooke describes Maud *as the loveliest of Tennyson's longer poems even as he mourns its jingoistic sentiments– not as faulty notions of war as the cure for a wounded hearth, but as faultily suggesting that the Crimean war could provide such a cure. In spite of its glorification of an unjust war, Brooke sees the monodrama s the poem of the broken heart, reaching the depths of sorrow at which beauty garbs the soul.*

Buckley, Jerome Hamilton. *"Maud." Tennyson: A Collection of Critical Essays.*
Ed. Elizabeth Francis. Englewood Cliffs: Prentice Hall, 1980. 156-62.
In this general introduction to the monodrama, Buckley describes the speaker of Maud *as a sensibility rather than an individual: a morbid soul akin to the Byronic hero and the protagonists of the Spasmodic closet dramas.* Maud *is upheld by Buckley as the most carefully constructed of Tennyson's longer works and a symbolist poem rather than a case history.*

---. *"The Spasmodic School. The Victorian Temper: A Study in Literary Culture.*
Cambridge: Harvard UP, 1951.
In this chapter, Buckley links Maud *to the Spasmodic closet dramas in form, theme, and substance, yet he then notes that it surpasses them in its ability to portray Tennyson's conflicting Romantic subjectivity and Victorian mistrust of it.*

Bucknill, John Charles. "Tennyson's *Maud and Other Poems." Asylum Journal of Mental Science* 2 (Oct. 1855): 95-104.
Bucknill suggests that Tennyson's poetry is more revealing of mental science than the work of those in the sciences, and that Maud, *an accurate portrait of psychological probabilities: of alienism, of pathology, and of delusion, is the history of a madman depicted by a master.*

Byatt, A.S. "The Lyric Structure of Tennyson's *Maud." The Major Victorian Poets: Reconsiderations.* Ed. Isobel Armstrong. London: Routledge, 1969.
69-92.
Byatt praises Tennyson's use of the lyric form to present emotion and sensual description.

Campbell, Matthew. *Rhythm and Will in Victorian Poetry.* Cambridge: Cambridge UP, 1999.
Campbell treats the inability to control language as the central theme of the poem, discussing language as it is used by the speaker to express consciousness and as a dominating system over which the speaker has little control.

Canon, J. "Editor's Tableau." *Genius of the West* 4 (Nov. 1855): 347-48.
This work briefly notes some of the conflicting critical reactions to Maud *without adding a judgment of its own.*

Chandler, Alice. "Tennyson's *Maud* and the Song of Songs" *Victorian Poetry* 7 (1969): 91-104.
Chandler links Maud *to the biblical* Song of Songs *in its plot, its imagery, its language, and in its presentation of a shulamite maiden whose purifying love leads the hero to righteousness.*

Clark, Barbara Anne Roberts. "Critical Annotations for Tennyson's *Maud*." Diss. U of Georgia, 1970.
In this detailed and admirable study, Clark offers full annotations for Maud, *including its stages of composition, its biographical and literary influences, Tennyson's comments about it, those of his peers, and those found in current scholarship. This work serves, in my opinion, as a prime example of the excellent, much needed work being done by graduate students in exploration of Tennyson's monodrama.*

Colley, Ann. *Tennyson and Madness*. Athens: U of Georgia P, 1983.
Treating the biographical influences on the poem, Colley sees the old grey wolf as representing Tennyson's father and supports Rader's linking of Maud *to Rosa Baring. Colley also links the love interest to the numerous descriptions of monomaniacs that were highlighted in nineteenth century treatises on insanity and thus refutes the criticism that denounces the ending of the poem as anything other than the product of a diseased mind.*

Collins, Joseph. "Tennyson and the Spasmodics." *Victorian Newsletter* 43 (Spring 1973): 24-28.
This in an important starting place for anyone who is trying to refute the supposed Spasmodic heritage of Maud. *One of the first, of a mere few, to oppose the link, Collins makes an excellent case for* Maud's *having little similarity to the careless and absurd Spasmodic dramas.*

Collins, Philip. *Reading Aloud: A Victorian Metier*. Tennyson Society Monographs 5. Lincoln: Tennyson Society, 1972.
Collins describes Tennyson's dramatic readings of Maud *and of other works.*

Collins, Winston. " *Maud*: Tennyson's Point of War." *The Tennyson Research Bulletin* 2 (1974): 126-28.
Collins suggests that Maud *was influenced by Lushington's 1854 sixpenny pamphlet of poems:* Points of War, *a copy of which was sent to Emily Tennyson in 1854. He notes that "The Muster of the Guards," in particular, is similar to* Maud *in thought, imagery, phrasing, and rhythm, and that the two works share the overall theme of peace as fraudulent and corrupting. Interestingly, Collins also notes that Ruskin praised these sentiments in* Maud, *and that Ruskin's 1865 lecture at the Royal Military Academy redelivered them.*

"Contemporary Poets." *Independent* 7 Feb. 1856: 48.
See Beetz: entry 422.

"Country Correspondence." *Crayon* 3 Oct. 1856: 314-16.
The editor describes a conversation he had with a friend, Miss Abbott, on a train. During their chat, she described the monodrama as the work in which Tennyson proves himself a master at revealing not merely a scene from nature, but the essence of that scene. Miss Abbott's impression is than in a stanza of Maud Tennyson better renders the feeling and essence of scenery than lesser poets are able to do in paragraphs.

Cox, Janice Bain. "Tennyson's *Maud* in the Framework of Spasmodic Poetry." Thesis. Georgia State, 1967.
Noting both similarities and points of divergence, Cox treats Maud as akin to the Spasmodic works but different from them primarily in degree. For example, she maintains that Maud's hero is similar to the Spasmodic heroes in his employment of the pathetic fallacy and heightened emotional life, that the monodrama as a whole, like the Spasmodic works, is dramatic in form but lacking in dramatic action, and that it is lengthy like a Spasmodic work but less epic and grandiose in scope.

Crawford, John. "A Unifying Element in Tennyson's *Maud*." *Victorian Poetry* 7 (1969): 64-66.
In this brief but interesting note, Crawford describes war as the unifying framework of Maud and ties to this framework the shifting flower imagery of the garden scene, particularly in the stanza of the garden scene in which the speaker's discussion moves from the red rose, to the white rose, to the larkspur. Crawford notes that the red and white of the rose, with the addition of the blue larkspur, present the British national colors and call to mind the Union Jack as it is carried into battle.

Culler, Dwight. *The Poetry of Tennyson*. New Haven: Yale UP, 1977.
In the chapter titled "Maud or the Madness" (90-213), Culler revisits the exploration he began in his 1975 article for PMLA.

---. "Monodrama and the Dramatic Monologue." *PMLA* 90 (1975): 366-85.
Culler begins by reminding his readers that the term "dramatic monologue" was not in use while the great Victorian works of the genre were being penned. He then describes early precursors to the form and its arrival in England. He notes that Mann was the first to apply the title "monodrama" to Maud, that it deserves such a title in spite of its introspective centered plot, and that its hero is similar to Hamlet in that he runs through a whole spectrum of emotions in a dramatic context.

Cunningham, James Vincent. "The Spasmodic School of Poetry." Diss. St. John's U, 1941.
Cunningham explores what he sees as the Spasmodic qualities Maud shares with the work of Sydney Dobell, Alexander Smith, and Phillip Bailey.

"Current Literature, English and Foreign." *Aberdeen Journal* 29 Aug. 1855: 6.
See Shannon page 415.

Curtis, George William. "Editor's Easy Chair." *Harpers Monthly Magazine* Oct. 1855: 701-06.
Curtis praises Tennyson for having justly decried a sham peace and refutes suggestions that he betrayed his country in doing so.

---. "Editor's Easy Chair." *Harper's Monthly Magazine* Jan. 1856: 262.
The editor briefly notes that, in spite of Maud's unfortunate and negative reception, he thinks it a fine and unique poem worthy of its author.

Dallas, Eneas Sweetland. *Times* [London] 25 Aug. 1855: 8-9.
A review of "Maud" and Other Poems. See Shannon page 417.

Davies, James. "Dylan Thomas' 'One Warm Saturday' and Tennyson's *Maud*." *Studies in Short Fiction* 14 (1977): 284-86.
Davies notes that the similarities between the works in question extend beyond a recital of the garden scene lyrics from Maud by a character in "One Warm Saturday." For example, Tennyson's lily and Jack of the alehouse bench show up in the Thomas piece, and the two works share isolated melancholic heroes threatened by competition from more wealthy suitors, as well as garden and grave motifs.

Davis, Lisa Hammontree. "Contemporary Social Issues in Tennyson's *Maud: A Monodrama*." Thesis. East Carolina U, 1989.
Davis' thesis is unique in that it treats the social ills featured at the heart of Maud: overcrowded living conditions, the adulteration of food and drugs, and the high child mortality rate that led to the distribution of burial fees.

Day, Aiden. "The Archetype that Waits: *The Lover's Tale, In Memoriam*, and *Maud*." *Tennyson: Seven Essays*. Ed. Phil Collins and Arthur William. New York: St. Martins, 1992. 76-101.
Day treats, as a common Tennysonian theme, looking outside the boundaries of the text, of language, and of consciousness for an archetype who can provide epistemological certainty. He notes that, in the "O that 'twere possible" lyric, and in Maud as a whole, we find a speaker who is haunted by the absence of a loved one. This haunting reveals a self-dissolving dependence on the archetypal waiting other, and his imagined union with this other signifies a further turn away from language and consciousness.

Dereli, Cynthia. "Tennyson's *Maud*: Ambiguity and the War Context." *Tennyson Research Bulletin* 7 (1997): 1-6.
Dereli here refutes comparisons made, by Schweik and Collins, respectively, of Maud's war theme to that found in Swayne's article "Peace and War" and the nationalistic poems of Henry and Franklin Lushington.

Dixon, Hepworth. Rev. of *Maud*, by Alfred Tennyson. *Athenaeum* 4 Aug. 1855: 893-95.
See Shannon page 415.

Drew, Philip. "Tennyson and the Dramatic Monologue: A Study of *Maud*."
Writers and Their Background: Tennyson. Ed. D Palmer. Athens: Ohio UP, 1973.
115-46.
*Drew explores the relationship of the poem's speaker to the author hiding behind his
mask and arrives at the conclusion that Tennyson employs the dramatic monologue
form as a facade, that it could be, in fact, argued that he wrote no dramatic
monologues which fully deserve the term, and that, in* Maud, *the dramatic cannot be
clearly distinguished from the confessional. Drew offers here, perhaps first, what
seems the current standard impression of Tennyson as a practitioner of the dramatic
monologue form. However, I recommend following any work on this topic with
Linda Hughes'* The Manyfacéd Glass: Tennyson's Dramatic Monologues, *a highly
informative and delightful study.*

Driskell, Leon Vinson. "Whitman and Tennyson: A Critical Study of *Song of
Myself* and *Maud*." Thesis. U of Georgia, 1956.
*Driskell compares the initial critical response to the two poems, noting that readers
accused both Tennyson and Whitman of writing poetry that lacked form, of being
guilty of what appeared an assault on middle class respectability, and of presenting
similarly unreadable work. Driskell's focus is a comparative study of secondary
explorations of* Song of Myself *and* Maud, *rather than on the primary sources
themselves.*

Dudley, Arthur. "La Poésie Anglais Depuis Shelley." *Revue des Deux Mondes* 15
(1856): 821-46.
Dudley describes Maud *as an insincere effort on Tennyson's part: the failed effort
of a poet past his prime. Dudley suggests that instead of being the master of emotion
as he was in* In Memoriam, *Tennyson is now mastered by his emotions.*

"Editor's Table." *Graham's Magazine* Jan. 1856: 71.
Amidst a discussion of Longfellow, the reviewer describes Maud *as the work in
which Tennyson most moves beyond the reach of rivals and imitators who try to
equal him in musical ability.*

"Editor's Table." *Graham's Magazine* Oct. 1855: 360-61.
*The editor praises Tennyson for the originality and honest but strikingly jingoistic
sentiments of* Maud.

Eidson, John Olin. *Tennyson in America: His Reputation and Influence from
1827-1858*. Athens: U of Georgia P, 1943.
Eidson's section on Maud *offers an excellent introduction to the monodrama's
reception in America.*

Elfenbein, Andrew. *Byron, Byronism, and the Victorians*. Diss. Yale, 1991. Ann
Arbor: UMI, 1993. 9221328.
Elfenbein suggests that with Maud *Tennyson embraced a Byronic tradition of poetry
about social issues that had been perpetuated by the Chartist and Spasmodic schools:
products of a political and social strain of Romanticism that Tennyson had earlier
rejected. This work is significant in that it notes Tennyson's debt to the Spasmodics*

95

as one engendered by the Spasmodics having kept Romanticism alive well past the death of Byron, and that they did so by tempering their Romantic flights with a serious look at social issues, which paved the way for Maud.

Eliot, George. "Belles-Lettres." *Westminster Review* 64 (Oct. 1855): 596-601.
This review faults Maud as having a morbid tone and morbid conclusion. Eliot describes the monodrama as a morbid collection of hateful and exaggerated conceits designed to express things better left unsaid.

Engbretsen, Nancy Martina. "Tennyson's Longer Narrative Poems: *The Princess, Maud,* and *Idylls of the King.*" Diss. New York U, 1964.
Engbretsen treats Maud as a pre-symbolist work in technique and as a forerunner of modernism in its presentation of moral and psychological dislocation.

Farrell, John P. "The Bride of Lammermoor as Oracular Text in Emily Bronte, Tennyson, and Hardy." *South Central Review: The Journal of the South Central Modern Language Association* 1.4 (Winter 1984): 53-63.
Farrell treats The Bride of Lammermoor's influence on Maud, Wuthering Heights, and Tess of the D'Urbervilles, particularly in their shared suggestion that alienating, dysfunctional, and incoherent social action is mirrored in the alienated, dysfunctional, and incoherent self. He sees Scott's novel as having pre-dated the social concerns in Maud and notes that they share the theme of following the war trumpet as a way of resolving the injustice done to one's patrimony.

"English and an American Poet." *American Phrenological Journal* 12 (Oct. 1855): 90-91.
In a brief but caustic review, Tennyson's "Maud" and Other Poems is described as a product of the school of poets that includes Alexander Smith, and a work of ennui and unnatural, shocking passions.

Fischler, Alan. "Love in the Garden: *Maud, Great Expectations,* and W. S. Gilbert's *Sweethearts.*" *SEL* 37 (1997): 763-81.
Fischler treats Maud as an example of how scientific concerns raised in the nineteenth century robbed the Victorians of their faith in Christianity and its symbols, highlighting the speaker's mistrust in God and the poem's Darwinian presentation of the garden as a sphere of death rather than of generation.

Flynn, Dennis. Tennyson's 'Old Rhyme': "A Tennyson Epigraph to *Maud?*" *TLS* 30 July 1999: 12.
Flynn provides an unpublished epigraph in proof-sheets to the 1856-edition of Maud.

Forester, John. "The Literary Examiner." *London Examiner* 4 Aug. 1855: 483-84. Rpt. in *Littell's Living Age* 15 Sept. 1855: 54-57.
Forester praises Maud for its ability to evoke emotions by revealing the essence of scenery and describes it as one of the most perfect examples of description's ability to evoke emotions. He sees Maud as a series of highly finished lyrics that leads the reader through a succession of moods, rather than as a dramatic, unified narrative.

Forman, Buxton. *Our Living Poets: An Essay in Criticism.* London, 1871.
Buxton praises Maud *as a modern, progressive, dramatic and original poem. He suggests the work is Tennyson's greatest accomplishment in form and metrics, and that it inspired Swinburne's lyricism: a relationship suggested and left undeveloped, but not absurd to contemplate. Forman suggests that the critical hostility directed toward* Maud *resulted from the sluggish indifference of the British toward anything disconnected from a lucrative peace and their distaste for even mildly unpleasant self portraits. Forman's overall evaluation of* Maud *is that it displays a facility with language previously absent in English literature.*

Fox, William Johnson. "The War Poetry of the Laureate." *Weekly Dispatch* 26
 Aug. 1855: 7.
See Shannon page 417.

Fredeman, William E. "Rossetti's Impromptu Portraits of Tennyson Reading
 Maud." *Burlington Magazine* Mar. 1964: 117-18 and 413.
Fredeman presents Rossetti's sketches of Tennyson reciting Maud *during a dinner party at the home of Robert Browning.*

Fulford, William. "Alfred Tennyson. An Essay in Three Parts. Part III: *Maud*, and
 Other Poems." *Oxford and Cambridge Magazine* 1.3 (Mar. 1856): 136-45.
Fulford chastises the critics who offer what he sees as shortsighted depreciation of Maud: *a work he thinks the finest in the English language. He then counters individually the points on which* Maud *is often faulted. For example, he notes that the poem should not be condemned for featuring an overly introspective hero since the poem as a whole is designed to expose and protest such introspection. Fulford also suggests that critics read too much of Tennyson's biography into the poem, and that Tennyson's autobiographical phase ended with* In Memoriam. *He finds in the hero a leaning toward bitter satire that nevertheless offers a humanistic and appropriate suggestion that we must answer our own ills and not look to science or God to address them.*

"Fusion of Authors and Publishers." *Home Journal* 13 Oct. 1855: N. pag.
The author briefly surveys various critical reactions to Maud *and links Tennyson to Byron in the derision and division his work inspired.*

Giordano, Frank. "The 'Red-Ribbed Hollow,' Suicide, and Part III in *Maud*."
 Notes and Queries 24 (1977): 402-04.
Giordano suggests that in his discussions of the red-ribbed hollow, the speaker subconsciously links Maud's *brother and father to his own father, and that this displacement is a sign of his subconscious need for self-destruction.*

Gladstone, William. Rev. of *"Maud" and Other Poems*, by Alfred Tennyson.
 New Quarterly Review 4 (Oct. 1855): 393-97.
Gladstone faults Maud *for having a vague story line and suggests that it may be progressive in its attempt to reveal a moral truth but that it nevertheless fails in doing so, that it lacks the music, sweetness, profundity of thought, and depth of passion which elsewhere distinguish Tennyson's poetry. The review concludes with an*

expressed hope that Tennyson's vanity will not render him indifferent to the defects of Maud*: defects that can only imperil his reputation.*

---. "Tennyson's Poems." *New Quarterly Review* 106 (Oct. 1859): 454-85.
Gladstone describes Maud *as the Tennysonian work least popular and least worthy of popularity: a work full of heavy dreaminess and obscurity that proves itself unworthy of the effort it takes to dispel this obscurity. The author resents what he sees as Tennyson's one dimensional portrait of England as a land of corrupt shopkeepers, and the work's jingoistic undertones, in Gladstone's impression, lack moderation and good sense. In particular, he finds absurd the presentation of war as a cure for Mammonism, noting that war is a vastly commercial enterprise. Gladstone's overall impression is that the work reveals a lack of loyalty, reverence, and discipline: common sentiments in the early reviews.*

Glanville, Priscilla June. *"*Maud *and the Spasmodics: A Vindication."* Thesis. U of South Florida, 1998.
Glanville refutes the notion that Maud *is of Spasmodic ancestry, in form, theme or content.*

Goslee, David F. "Fairer than Aught in the World Beside: The Speaker's Invocation of Maud." *Victorian Poetry* 23 (1985): 391-402.
This very interesting article deals with the central them of love in the monodrama, addressing the problematic status of Maud *as a love poem: an issue that surfaces each time we find the garden scene excerpted in collections of love sonnets. Goslee makes the interesting observation that the speaker's madness does not negate, but rather enhances, the depth and poignancy of his love for Maud. For example, his language in the garden scene reveals the fact that, subconsciously at least, he associates their love with death. How might such a passage be considered a tribute to love? What substantiates the theme of love in the work is that fact that when the speaker creates the world around him in his mind, his love interest surfaces not even amidst but particularly amidst, the forces at odds with love itself.*

Haigh, Warren. "A study comparing the heroes of *A Life-Drama*, *Balder* and *Maud*." Thesis. Northern State College, 1969.
Haigh likens the supposed conversion of the monodrama's hero to the redemption of Smith's Walter and Dobell's Balder.

Hale, Edward Everett. Rev. of *Maud*, by Alfred Tennyson. *North American Review* 81 (Oct. 1855): 544-46.
Hale suggests that the monodrama is fresh, unique, and musical, and that its finest passages are those which precede the ending, which Hale believes was added somewhat clumsily after Tennyson's initial enthusiasm for the poem had waned.

Hargrave, Harry. "Tennyson's 'Little *Hamlet*': Shakespearean Parallels in *Maud*." *A Fair Day in the Affections: Literary Essays in Honor of Robert B. White, Jr.* Durant, Jack, Thomas Hester, and Robert Tilman, eds. Raleigh: Winston, 1980. 151-58.

In this brief but important article, Hargrave treats similarities between the heroes and overall themes presented in Maud *and Shakespeare's* Hamlet, *including: the melancholic, philosophical, and suicidal nature of the heroes, both of whom lost a father to greed and avarice, and the overall themes of civil war, madness, and consuming nature.*

Harrison, Antony H. "Irony in Tennyson's Little *Hamlet*." *Journal of General Education* 32 (1981): 271-86.

Harrison notes that clear similarities exist between the speaker of Maud, Shakespeare's Hamlet, and the Spasmodic protagonists. However, he suggests that Tennyson, aware of such similarities, developed them in order to highlight the deficiencies of the Spasmodic school while celebrating the dramatic irony of Shakespeare. After discussing similarities ,in plot and characterization, between Maud *and* Hamlet, *Harrison treats in detail the forms of irony Tennyson employs in his monodrama: irony verbal, dramatic, and situational. This extensive use of irony, Harrison concludes, distinguished Tennyson's work from the inferior Spasmodic poetry it superficially resembles, which Harrison sees as Tennyson's conscious attempt to preserve the literary standards of his age.*

Harrison, Thomas P. "Tennyson's *Maud* and Shakespeare." *Shakespeare Association Bulletin* 17 (1942): 80-85.

Harrison briefly notes similarities between the speaker of Maud *and Shakespeare's Hamlet: both melancholic, suicidal heroes, and affirms that the two works share the overall theme of civil war. However, he then suggests that these similarities end in the fifth section of Part I, after which* Maud *is more akin to* Romeo *and* Juliet *and* King Lear.

Hendrickson, L. Review of *Maud*, by Alfred Tennyson. *National Quarterly Review* 5 (June 1862): 76-82.

Hendrickson suggests that the poem offers slight and disjointed action but affirms that the morbidity of the monodrama and its speaker accurately mirror that of the age and that this morbidity may be conquered in the actual world, as it is in the poem, through action.

Hinton, Ernestine Gibson. "Technique in Tennyson's *Maud*." Diss. U of Georgia, 1974.

In a broad but general new critical reading of Maud, *Hinton treats the devices— such as metrics, psychology, use of time and transition, and archetypal links— through which Tennyson makes of his monodrama a character-centered organic whole.*

H. J. "A Criticism Comprehensive and Suggestive." *Oxford Chronicle* 1 Sept. 1855: 6.

See Beetz: entry 367.

Hoge, James. "Jowett on Tennyson's *Maud*: A New Letter." *Notes and Queries* 24 (1977): 16-18.
Hoge quotes Jowett's letter to Tennyson, in which he advises the poet on how to respond to the poem's detractors.

Holloway, John. *The Proud Knowledge: Poetry, Insight and the Self, 1620-1920.* London: Routledge, 1977.
Holloway's clear and informative work describes Maud *as a dynastic poem in that it takes for granted expectations about how a man's life is related to his familial situation, and as Tennyson's "mid-Victorian novel": akin to* The Mill on the Floss, Wuthering Heights, *and* Jane Eyre *in its panoramic depictions of pastoral life, dynastic intricacies, and struggle between sexual feeling and social responsibility. At the same time, it offers a modern crisis of personality and exploration of a self fulfilled through integration with others, and with environment. Holloway sees* Maud, *in its metrical eminence and its use of the mileau and plot of a major novel, as one of the most original and ambitious English poems of the nineteenth century.*

-Horvathy, Eva Maria. *The Heirs to Madness: Tennyson's Distraught Speakers.* Diss. Miami U, 1982. Ann Arbor: UMI. 1983. 5227799.
Horvathy treats the hero of Maud *as the victim of an inherited, internal melancholy and as a filter to the moral madness of his age. Thus she refutes, by implication, the suggestion that Tennyson created in him a too melancholic, too caustic hero.*

Houghton, Walter and Stange, Robert, eds. *Victorian Poetry and Poetics.* Cambridge: Houghton, 1959.
Links Maud *to the Spasmodic closet dramas on page 7.*

Howard, Francesca Spenser. "The Theme of Materialism in Tennyson's *Maud*." Thesis. Tulane, 1955.

Howe, Merrill Levi. "Dante Gabriel Rossetti's Comments on *Maud*." *Modern Language Notes* 49 (1934): 290-293.
Howe describes Rossetti's letters to Allingham about Tennyson's recital of Maud *and his reaction to the poem's severe criticism.*

Hughes, Linda K. "From Parlor to Concert Hall: Arthur Somervell's Song-Cycle on Tennyson's *Maud*." *Victorian Studies* 30 (1986): 113-29. Rpt. in *The Lost Chord: Essays on Victorian Music.* Ed. Nicholas Temperley. Bloomington: Indiana UP, 1989. 102-18.
Hughes discusses Sommervell's song cycle as a melding of Victorian and Modern music.

---. *The Manyfacéd Glass: Tennyson's Dramatic Monologues.* Athens: Ohio UP, 1987.
This is one of the finest books in recent Tennyson scholarship. In clear, poignant, beautiful prose– prose fit to describe the work of England's most mellifluous poet– Hughes describes Maud *as a dramatic monologue of consciousness and as a rendering of a fluctuating consciousness through the sequencing of lyrics: a device*

Tennyson employed earlier with In Memoriam. *Taken as whole, Hughes' work brilliantly traces the evolution of Tennyson's use of the dramatic monologue of consciousness. From start to finish,* The Manyfacéd Glass *is a delight to read and a necessity for any serious student of the dramatic monologue.*

Hunter, Paul Curwood. "Verification and Structure in Tennyson's *Maud.*" Thesis. U of Cincinnati, 1966.
Hunter treats Maud*'s metrics and imagery, the relation of its lines and stanzas to mood, and the dramatic tone of its words and repetitive phrasing.*

Inglesfield, Robert. "Tennyson's 'Come into the Garden, Maud' and the 'Song of Solomon.'" *Victorian Poetry* 37 (1999): 121-123.
Providing another tie between Maud *and the* Song of Songs, *Inglesfield links the rhetoric and flower imagery found in* Maud*'s garden scene at the end of Part I to its biblical predecessor.*

Johnson, Christopher. "Speech and Violence in Tennyson's *Maud.*"*Essays in Criticism: A Quarterly Journal of Literary Criticism* 47 (1997): 33-61.
Treating language as necessarily false and falsehood as a form of violence, Johnson explores the poem's central link between speech and violence.

Johnson, E.D.H. "The Lily and the Rose: Symbolic Meaning in Tennyson's *Maud.*" *PMLA* 64 (1949): 122-27.
Johnson treats the monodrama's symbolic presentation of purity and passion.

Kang, Sang Deok. *Tennyson's Lyricism: The Aesthetic of Sorrow.* Diss. University of North Texas, 1993. Ann Arbor: UMI, 1993. 9326637.
Kang focuses on the monodrama's portrayal of grief and the means of overcoming it

Kendall, J. L. "Gem Imagery in Tennyson's *Maud.*" *Victorian Poetry* 17 (1979):389-94.   •
Kendall raises the interesting point that the speaker, in using gem imagery to describe Maud, associates himself with the luxury and materialism he claims to be at odds with, and that it reaches its height in connection with Maud's brother. Thus, the speaker's use of gem imagery reveals the desires and fixations he doesn't reveal even to himself, and suggests that he is not so much at odds with the sultans of the world as he is eager to be a sultan himself. His references to stone similarly reveals his own fixation with death, and gems and stone together purify that death.

Kenig, Lea."Tennyson's *Maud* and the Betrayal of Reason." Diss. Columbia, 1979.
Kenig provides a study of madness and form. See Beetz, entry 4912

Kennedy, Ian. "The Crisis of Language in Tennyson's *Maud.*" *Texas Studies in Literature and Language: A Journal of the Humanities* 19 (1977): 161-78.
Kennedy examines the monodrama's theme of the inability to convey meaning through language, which leads to a breakdown of both.

Killham, John. "Tennyson's *Maud*: the Function of the Imagery." *Critical Essays on the Poetry of Tennyson*. Comp. and ed. John Killham. New York: Barnes & Noble, 1960. 219-38.

Killham interestingly proposes that psychoanalytical readings of Maud *are based more on the reader's judgment of war rather than that of the protagonist, and that a purely historical reading of the poem suffers from the historical judgment of the Crimean war. Hence, he argues for a non-ideological reading of the poem's imagery: imagery of plants, animals and stones, brought to life by sound and color, and carried by dramatic movement from one lyric to another.*

Kincaid, James. *Tennyson's Major Poems: The Comic and Ironic Patterns*. New Haven: Yale UP, 1975.

Kincaid treats Maud *as a work in which opposing forces work, without negating one another, to demand contradictory but equal responses, unsettling the speaker through complexity.*

Kingsley, Charles. "Tennyson's *Maud*." *Fraser's Magazine* Sept. 1855: 264-73.

After refuting the critics who describe the monodrama as faultily constructed and immoral, Kingsley praises Maud *for its accurate and timely portrait of madness and cites it as evidence that Tennyson deserves his position as the only great poet of the day. He also describes the outpouring of criticism against the jingoism in* Maud *as evidence of how much England is in need of the call to action the poem concludes with.*

Kirkwood, Kenneth P. *"Maud": An Essay on Tennyson's Poem*. Ottawa: LeDroit, 1951.

See Beetz: entry 3480.

Kozicki, Henry. *Tennyson and Clio: History in the Major Poems*. Baltimore: John Hopkins UP, 1979.

Kozicki makes an interesting parallel between Maud *and the* Idylls of the King*, suggesting that the civil war that beset Camelot is highlighted in the monodrama, and that the hero of* Maud *is akin to Merlin entombed by his Vivien and made a scapegoat for his increasingly sensual and selfish age.*

Kurata, Marilyn J. "A Juggle Born of the Brain: A New Reading of *Maud*." *Victorian Poetry* 21 (1983): 369-78.

Kurata suggests that the speaker's relationship with Maud may be entirely the fabrication of his diseased mind.

Lai, Nam Chen. "In the Moated Grange: Madness and Love in Tennyson's Poetry." Diss. Miami U, 1982.

Lai treats the relationships between love and sexuality and madness and redemption, exploring Maud *as Tennyson's perhaps unintentionally ironic suggestion that love relied on to bridge the gap between our base and heroic nature often proves ultimately destructive.*

Lamb, John. *Imaginative Conversion: Tennyson's Use of His Literary Heritage.* Diss. New York U, 1986. Ann Arbor: UMI. 1986. 8706754.
Lamb treats Maud *as modern in its focus on consciousness.*

Langford, Thomas A. "The 'Phases of Passion' in Tennyson's *Maud.*" *South Central Bulletin* 30 (1970): 204-08.
Langford treats the monodrama's nature imagery: flowers, colors, animals and stones, as markers of shifts in the speaker's consciousness.

Langstaff, Eleanor. *The Desacralization of Metaphor in Nineteenth-Century English Poetry: The use of War Metaphor in" Sordello" and "Maud."* Diss. City U of New York, 1998. Ann Arbor: UMI, 1999. 9838822.
Langstaff explores Maud *as evidence of the fact that in the Victorian age, warfare had become separated from God's agency.*

Latane, David. "Spasmodic Poetry." *Victorian Britain: An Encyclopedia.* Ed. Sally Mitchell. New York: Garland, 1988. 358.
Latane suggests that the Spasmodic closet dramas influenced Tennyson's Maud *and E.B. Browning's* Aurora Leigh.

"The Laureate's View of War." *Punch* 18 Aug. 1855: 69.
This brief, witty poem is a parody set in the style form of Maud. *Its main purpose is to mock Tennyson's supposed jingoism and* Maud*'s presentation of war as a cure for Mammonism.*

Lavabre, Simone. "Une Lecture de *Maud.*" *Caliban* 7 (1970): 25-34.
See Beetz: entry 4257.

Lee, Brian S. "The Martial Conclusions of Tennyson's *Maud* and Lawrence's *England, My England.*" *University of Cape Town Studies in English* 12 (Oct.1982): 19-37.
Lee treats the theme of war as manifested in Maud *and* England My England. *In doing so, he explores Tennyson's monodrama as dramatic rather than autobiographical. Lee concludes that Tennyson's hero is not a filter for jingoistic propaganda but an unstable individual who finds in patriotism a release for once suppressed violent impulses.*

Lee, William Lamborn. *Interpreting Insane Characters in* King Lear, The Duchess of Malfi, Rasselas, Maud, *and* As I Lay Dying *Toward a Theory.* Diss. Yale, 1980. Ann Arbor: UMI. 1980. 8025210.
Lee suggests that in Maud *Tennyson paints an accurate portrait of madness yet consciously makes ambiguous the speaker's descent to and from this madness in order to highlight the relationship between madness, perception, and social mores.*

Levi, Peter. *Tennyson.* London: Macmillan, 1993.
In his chapter on Maud, *Levi's biography picks up with Tennyson's marriage to Emily and concludes with the September after* Maud*'s publication. In this chapter, among other relationships, he briefly describes that which links the monodrama and the Spasmodic poets.*

"Literary and Artistic Gossip." *Weekly Chronicle* 4 Aug. 1855: 489.
See Shannon page 417.

"Literature of the Month." *Birmingham Journal* 11 Aug. 1855, supplement: 3.
*Reviews "Maud" and Other Poems and describes Maud as too mystic, too incomplete,
and too involved to be understood and appreciated by its readers. The reviewer
suggests that Tennyson, in creating Maud, displayed sublime indifference toward its
readability and thus created a confusing and disjointed narrative that overshadows
the work's musical merits.*

Lougy, Robert E. "The Sounds and Silence of Madness: Language as Theme in
   Tennyson's *Maud.*" *Victorian Poetry* 22 (1984): 407-26.
*Lougy treats Maud as a poem about fragmentation itself and explores its slips
between language and meaning, between sanity and madness, between sound and
silence, and between reality and imagination.*

Lounsbury, Thomas R. "Tennyson's *Maud* as a Work of Art." *Yale Literary
   Magazine* Dec. 1858: 89-98.
*This review describes Maud as more than a love story and more than a jingoistic
invective against civil war, linking it instead to the common Victorian theme of
progress through action. Lounsbury begins by describing the monodrama as an
accurate psychological portrait of many idealistic young men in nineteenth century
England. He sees it as the product of an age in which passion, restless longing, and
morbid excitement were common among one sided idealists. Such states, Lounsbury
notes, form a part of the history of every enthusiastic man. Answering common
themes in Maud scholarship of the 1850s, he also notes that the ending of Maud does
not provide a glorification of war in general, but war as an agent of civil liberty, as
a cure for despotism, and as the herald of a more glorious civilization. Nor does it
provide a denunciation of peace in general, but of peace as far as it leads to a giving
in to tyranny and a hindrance to advancement. Lounsbury sees the work's overall
theme as a call to trade the sordid interests of the present for a prostration and duty
that will herald future prosperity. He also sees its overall structure as one of a
unified work of art, rather than a string of pearls: the metaphor around which the
review is titled.*

Luce, Morton. *New Studies in Tennyson: Including a Commentary on "Maud."*
   Clifton, 1893.
*Luce's very negative analysis of Maud is designed to refute Mann's vindication of it.
Luce finds too much of Tennyson: the angry prophet, in the poem to agree with
Mann's assertion that the work is a dramatic fiction. Instead, he sees the narrator as
a mask behind which Tennyson rages. In this, according to Luce, the hero is indeed
akin to Shakespeare's Hamlet, who suffered Shakespeare's sorrows and teetered on
madness lest he reflect the artist too closely. Luce doesn't agree with Mann's
attributing the speaker's violent impulses to madness because he sees the speaker as
sane yet as violent as ever at the end of the poem. Luce's global evaluation of the
poem is that the lovely "O that 'twere possible" germ printed in the Tribute was*

ruined in the process through which it became Maud*: Tennyson's finest poetry but worst poem.*

MacDonald, Andrew. "Dramatic Unity in Tennyson's *Maud*." Thesis. Tulane, 1966.

Macdonald explores elements of the poem that make it clearly dramatic and lend it unity: the in medias res beginning, the way it forces participation from its "audience," the malcontent, cynical personality of its speaker, the dramatic exchange of its characters, and its unifying symbolism. Additionally, he refutes the common suggestion that the speaker's ravings are the totally illogical products of madness, instead exploring the speaker's outbursts as a systematic, active engagement of the world through the pathetic fallacy. MacDonald also treats Maud *as a dramatic monologue in its objectivity, internal drama, oral realism, and psychological self-revelation.*

Machann, Clinton. "Tennyson's King Arthur and the Violence of Manliness." *Victorian Poetry* 38 (2000) 199-226.

Machann briefly describes Maud *as Tennyson's most explicit exploration of male madness and a work in which irrational and destructive male violence is closely associated with male sexuality.*

Mann, Robert J. *Tennyson's "Maud" Vindicated: An Explanatory Essay.* London, 1856.

In the work of appreciative criticism Tennyson himself is likely to have approved before its publication, Mann challenges those early critics who were inclined to see Tennyson's monodrama as autobiographical and explores the monodrama as a clearly dramatic fiction. In the process of championing Maud*'s status as a drama, he suggests that prior to its publication the power of language to render emotion had never been so magically proved, and that its presentation of the holy power of love proves that Tennyson is a teacher as much as he is a musician.*

Marshall, George O. "An Incident from Carlyle in Tennyson's *Maud*." *Notes and Queries* 6 (1959): 77-78.

Marshall links Maud*'s presentation of Mammonite mothers to a similar occurrence in Book II of Carlyle's* Past and Present.

---. "Tennyson's 'Oh! That 'Twere Possible': A Link Between *In Memoriam* and *Maud*." *PMLA* 78 (1963): 225-229.

Marshall suggests that the "Oh! that 'Twere Possible" germ published in the Tribute *is similar to* In Memoriam *in its speaker's hope to embrace an archetype who waits for him in the sky, and he notes that in the* Tribute *germ of* Maud *there was no suggestion that the apparition was anything other then the speaker's grief over the death of a beloved. Marshall gathers from this the theory that by expressing his despair over the death of Arthur Hallam in terms of a man's love for a woman Tennyson was trying to ease his anguish by objectifying it, making the death of Hallam the link between* Maud *and* In Memoriam.

Massey, Gerald. Rev. of Maud, by Alfred Tennyson. *Edinburgh News and Literary Chronicle* 28 July 1855: 7.
See Shannon page 415.

---. "The Poetry of Alfred Tennyson." *Eclectic Magazine of Foreign Literature, Science and Art* (Sept 1855): 616-28.
Praising Maud *indirectly in this lengthy and stylistically beautiful review, Massey lauds English efforts in the Crimean war and notes that such exploits not only cleared the lethargic fog from English society but also produced great work by Tennyson. Tennyson is then described as one of English literature's titans, along with Shelley, Byron, and Wordsworth, who were led to magnificent work by the French Revolution.*
Rev. of *Maud*, by Alfred Tennyson. *Albion*. 1 Sept. 1855: 417.
Describes the monodrama as a morbid, misanthropical, episodic tale relieved by gushes of genuine and exquisite poetry.

Rev. of Maud, by Alfred Tennyson. *Atlas* 4 Aug. 1855: 499.
See Shannon page 415.

Rev. of Maud, by Alfred Tennyson. *Banner of Ulster* [Belfast] 6 Sept. 1855: 4.
See Shannon page 415.

Rev. of Maud, by Alfred Tennyson. *Brechin Advertiser* 4 Sept. 1855: 4.
See Shannon page 415.

Rev. of *"Maud, and Other Poems*, by Alfred Tennyson. *British Quarterly Review* 22 (Oct. 1855): 467-98.
The reviewer praises the originality of Maud *'s metrical experiments and refutes the theory that the poem reveals Tennyson's jingoism and morbidity. Rather, the reviewer suggests that* Maud *'s metrics reveal, in themselves, the fact that their author is of a higher and nobler nature than most individuals, and that they alone negate any charges of immorality and jingoism leveled against Tennyson.*

Rev. of *"Maud" and Other Poems*, by Alfred Tennyson. *Eclectic Review* 102 (Nov. 1855): 568-75.
This review faults Maud *for unmelodious lyricism and suggests that, in writing it, Tennyson clearly intended to shock rather than to please. The review also somewhat snobbishly faults the poem for lapsing into language better suited to a farmer than a poet, citing the use of "moor land" for "moorland" as evidence, and for lapsing into "twaddle": a type of verse this bibliographer would not presume to define for you. The overall impression expressed here is that the monodrama is a bold but unsuccessful attempt to combine the lyric and dramatic modes.*

Rev. of *"Maud" and Other Poems*, by Alfred Tennyson. *Family Friend* Sept 1855: 251-54.
This very negative review cites Maud *as an example of wild, visionary abuse that glorifies war with a virulence and coarseness previously unmet in literature. The verse is described as rabid, the story as weakly constructed and autobiographical, and the work on the whole as fiercely antagonistic.*

Rev. of *"Maud" and Other Poems*, by Alfred Tennyson. *John Bull* 18 Aug. 1855: 523-24.

The reviewer praises Maud *as both a series of light, airy sketches and a work of high moral aim delivered with a stern tone: a tale of love full of both sweetness and sadness.*

Rev. of *"Maud" and other Poems*, by Alfred Tennyson. *Knickerbocker* 46 (Nov. 1855): 525-26.

Describes Maud *as a great disappointment and a morbid, misanthropic, auto-biographical string of episodes that occasionally break into decent poetry.*

Rev. of *"Maud," and Other Poems*, by Alfred Tennyson. *Press* 11 Aug. 1855: 764-65.

In one of the most sarcastic and caustic of Maud*'s early reviews, the reviewer accuses Tennyson of writing unintelligibly, describes* Maud *as a sickly poem, suggests that those who appreciate it are inclined to like poetry more when they appreciate it less, and cites existence of such fans as evidence that the age itself is diseased. Taken at its best, the reviewer notes, the monodrama is a strain of incoherent sentiment and disordered fantasy: the brain fever of a lovesick youth with the measles. The review closes with the reviewer's wish that Tennyson fall gently from his pedestal.*

Rev. of *"Maud" and Other Poems*, by Alfred Tennyson. *Rambler: A Catholic Journal and Review* 4 (Sept. 1855): 240-42.

The reviewer briefly describes Maud *as a series of autobiographical pictures in which the verse, melody, and diction vary with the speaker's states of mind.*

Rev. of *"Maud" and Other Poems*, by Alfred Tennyson. *Spectator* 4 Oct. 1855: 813-14. Rpt. in *Littell's Living Age* 15 Sept. 1855: 57-61.

The reviewer quite reasonably notes that the monodrama is not designed for those who look to poetry for amusement without reflection or for stimulation without imagination and morality. He or she then describes Maud *as a series of fragments from a poetical diary, fragments perfectly intelligible, and clearly autobiographical yet rendered with a dramatic force not found in the poet's previous work. This review also makes a comparison of* Maud *to Goethe's* Faust *in its depth of passion and pathos.*

Rev. of *"Maud" and Other Poems*, by Alfred Tennyson. *Tait's Edinburgh Magazine* Sept 1855: 531-39.

This review describes Maud *as a love story, slight in fabric and told in snatches of melody, over which is grafted an unintelligible and unsavory anti-peace moral, and as an example of the fact that Tennyson knows as little about war as does Mr. Bright, whom the narrative impales. The reviewer concedes that as Queen Victoria's laureate, Tennyson must keep a "war trumpet" but that his is a very ineffective trumpet, and one that sounded too late in* Maud, *as the war furor of England had largely subsided. The reviewer concludes that* Maud *makes evident the fact that Tennyson is a poet of beauty rather than of philosophy who should scorn the latter for the former.*

Rev. of *"Maud" and Other Poems*, by Alfred Tennyson. *Times* [New York] 13
Nov. 1855: 2-3.
In this quite divided review, Maud *is described as being faulty only when compared
to the best of Tennyson's previous work, and the suggestion is made that if it had been
written by another poet it would have been hailed a success.* Maud *is then described
as a dramatic poem that employs mood better than it does the sequential framework
needed for dramatic tension. Its lyrical composition is praised, yet, at the same time,
the work as a whole is criticized for its forced moral, its lack of coherency, and its
Spasmodic-like plot.*

Rev. of *Maud*, by Alfred Tennyson. *Ayr Observer* 7 Aug. 1855: 2.
See Shannon page 415.

Rev. of *Maud*, by Alfred Tennyson. *Bath Chronicle* 9 Aug. 1855: 3.
Extracted from an August 4 review in Athenaeum. *See Shannon page 415.*

Rev. of *Maud*, by Alfred Tennyson. *Biblioteca Sacra* 12 (Oct. 1855): 851.
A brief notice of Maud *as inferior to "The Princess."*

Rev. of *Maud*, by Alfred Tennyson. *Court Journal* 11 Aug. 1855: 539.
See Shannon page 415.

Rev. of Maud, by Alfred Tennyson. *Christian Reformer* 11 (Oct. 1855): 602-13.
See Shannon page 415.

Rev. of Maud, by Alfred Tennyson. *Daily Express* [Edinburgh] 11 Aug. 1855: 4.
See Shannon page 415.

Rev. of *Maud*, by Alfred Tennyson. *Daily News* 17 Aug. 1855: 2.
See Shannon page 415.

Rev. of *Maud*, by Alfred Tennyson. *Daily Post* [Liverpool] 2 Aug. 1855: 6.
See Shannon page 415.

Rev. of *Maud*, by Alfred Tennyson. *Dumfries-shire and Galloway Herald and
Register* 3 Aug 1855: 1.
See Shannon page 415.

Rev. of *Maud*, by Alfred Tennyson. *Dundee, Perth, and Cupar Advertiser* 31 July.
1855: 2.
See Shannon page 415.

Rev. of Maud, by Alfred Tennyson. *Dundee and Perth Saturday Post* 6 Oct. 1855:
4.
See Shannon page 415.

Rev. of Maud, by Alfred Tennyson. *Ecclesiastic and Theologian* 17 (Sept. 1855):
431-36.
Mentioned in Shannon 415 and in Beetz: entry 347.

Rev. of Maud, by Alfred Tennyson *Edinburgh Advertiser* 21 Sept. 1855: 3.
A brief review of Maud *noted in Shannon 416 and in Beetz: entry 349.*

Rev. of Maud, by Alfred Tennyson. *Edinburgh Evening Courant* 2 Aug. 1855: 3.
A brief review of Maud *noted in Shannon 416 and in Beetz: entry 350.*

Rev. of *Maud*, by Alfred Tennyson. *Era* 9 Sept. 1855: 10.
A notice mentioned in a review of the poetical works of William Lisle Bowles. See Shannon page 415.

Rev. of *Maud*, by Alfred Tennyson. *General Advertiser* [Dublin] 15 Sep. 1855: 3.
Abstracted from a September review in Fraser's Magazine. *.See Shannon page 416.*

Rev. of *Maud*, by Alfred Tennyson. *Globe* 18 Oct. 1855: 1.
See Shannon page 416.

Rev. of *Maud*, by Alfred Tennyson. *Graham's Magazine* 47 (Oct. 1855): 371-72.
The reviewer accurately notes that those readers of Tennyson who admire him most for the daintiness of his melodies will be disappointed with Maud. *He then affirms that the work is full of genius and power and that its hero's ravings are morally false but artistically appropriate, given his misery and misanthropy.*

Rev. of *Maud*, by Alfred Tennyson. *Greenock Advertiser* 14 Aug. 1855: 4.
See Shannon page 416

Rev. of Maud, by Alfred Tennyson. *Guardian* [London] 29 Aug. 1855: 664.
This very negative review calls Maud *a dreary, inharmonious, and vague poem in the Spasmodic tradition and cites it as evidence that the Poet Laureate had regressed to the worst affectations and extravagances of his youth. The reviewer admires the hero's yearning fondness for his childhood sweetheart but finds his madness coarsely and disagreeably presented.*

Rev. of *Maud*, by Alfred Tennyson. *Illustrated Times* [London] 4 Aug. 1855: 142-43.
The reviewer praises Maud *for containing Tennysonian metrical beauty in full flower and for its daring allusions to social phenomena of the day. Its hero is described as a slightly morbid young man who nevertheless appropriately looks to war to resolve political and moral stagnation and shares even the most morbid of his sentiments in lovely poetic flights.*

Rev. of *Maud*, by Alfred Tennyson. *Inquirer* 1 Sept. 1855: 546-47.
Mentioned in Shannon page 416 and in Beetz: entry 374.

Rev. of Maud, by Alfred Tennyson. *Inverness Courier* 2 Aug. 1855: 2.
See Shannon page 416.

Rev. of *Maud*, by Alfred Tennyson. *Lady's Newspaper* 4 Aug. 1855: 75.
See Shannon page 416.

Rev of *Maud*, by Alfred Tennyson. *Leeds Mercury* [London] 11 Aug. 1855: 7.
The reviewer begins by noting the conflicting impressions of Maud *found in prominent contemporary journals and then agrees with those that see the monodrama as a work of rich and varied beauty well worth the efforts of its creator.*

Rev. of Maud, by Alfred Tennyson. *Literary Gazette* 4 Aug. 1855: 483-84.
See Shannon page 416.

Rev of *Maud,* by Alfred Tennyson. *London Quarterly Review* 5 (Oct. 1855): 213-29.
Praises Maud *for its originality and objects to the comparison of* Maud *with the inferior and imitative work of the Spasmodic poets.*

Rev of *Maud,* by Alfred Tennyson. *London University Magazine* 1 May 1856: 1-11.
The reviewer praises Maud *for presenting themes and personalities common to the age.*

Rev. of *Maud*, by Alfred Tennyson. *Magnet* 17 Sept. 1855: 6.
An abridged version of a September 1st review in Morning Post. *See Shannon page 416.*

Rev. of *Maud*, by Alfred Tennyson. *Manchester Examiner and Times* 7 Aug. 1855: 2.
See Shannon page 416 and Beetz: entry 387.

Rev of *Maud,* by Alfred Tennyson. *Monthly Review of Literature, Science, and Art.* 1 (Jan. 1856): 19-24.
See Beetz: entry 433.

Rev. of *Maud*, by Alfred Tennyson. *Morning Herald* 22 Aug. 1855: 7.
See Shannon page 416.

"The Cure for Mammonism." *Morning Post* 2 Aug. 1855: 6.
See Shannon page 416.

Rev. of *Maud*, by Alfred Tennyson. *National Magazine* Oct. 1856: 3-5.
A bibliographic and critical article. See Shannon page 417.

Rev. of *Maud*, by Alfred Tennyson. *News of the World* 16 Sept. 1855: 6.
An abridged version of the Morning Post *September 1ˢᵗ review. See Shannon page 416.*

Rev. of *Maud*, by Alfred Tennyson. *Northern Whig* [Belfast] 7 Aug. 1855: 4.
A reprint of an August 4ᵗʰ review in Spectator. *See Shannon page 416.*

Rev. of *Maud*, by Alfred Tennyson. *Overland Mail* 10 Aug. 1855: 82.
See Shannon page 416.

Rev. of *Maud*, by Alfred Tennyson. *Oxford University Herald* 18 Aug. 1855: 14.
See Shannon page 416.

Rev. of *Maud,* by Alfred Tennyson. *Perthshire Courier* 30 Aug 1855: 4.
See Shannon page 416.

Rev. of Maud, by Alfred Tennyson. *Revue Britannique* Sept. 1855: 234-36.
The reviewer accuses Tennyson, the poet of sweet songs, of rashly blowing the war trumpet in Maud*'s prologue and epilogue.*

Rev. of Maud, by Alfred Tennyson. *Saturday Evening Post* 8 Sept. 1855: N. pag.
See Beetz: entry 400.

Rev. of Maud, by Alfred Tennyson. *Scotsman* 29 Aug. 1855: 3.
See Shannon page 416.

Rev. of *Maud,* by Alfred Tennyson. *Spectator* 3 Sept. 1892: 325-27.
See Beetz: entry 1598.

Rev. of Maud, by Alfred Tennyson. *Sun* 27 Aug. 1855: 3.
Listed in Shannon on page 417, and in Beetz: entry 405.

Rev. of Maud, by Alfred Tennyson. *Tablet* [Dublin] 25 Aug. 1855: 539.
See Shannon page 417.

Mermin, Dorothy M. "Tennyson's *Maud*; A Thematic Analysis." *Texas Studies in Literature and Language: A Journal of the Humanities* 15 (1973): 267-78.
Mermin refutes contemporary appraisals of Maud *as primarily biographical or simply a collection of disjointed lyrics. Highlighting the work's complex thematic structure, she traces through the narrator's madness and melancholy an inability to let go of the past and come to terms with loss.*

Miller, Hugh. *Witness* [Edinburgh] 1 Sept. 1855: 2.
See Shannon page 417.

Milne, Fred L. "Yeats' 'The Cap and Bells': A Probable Indebtedness to Tennyson's *Maud.*" *Ariel: A Review of International English Literature* 3.3 (1972): 69-79.
Milne suggests that in details of imagery, setting, dramatic action, and theme Yeats' work may be indebted to Maud*: the product of Tennyson's middle period, and a period that Yeats, on the whole, was not favorably impressed with. For example, Milne links the monodrama's flower imagery to Yeats'* The Shadowy Waters, *the hero of the monodrama's passionate love for Maud to that of Yeats for Maud Gonne, and the monodrama's image of the cap and bells of a fool to similar images in Yeats' "The Queen and the Fool" and* A Vision. *Milne also notes that Tennyson's* Maud *and Yeats' "The Cap and Bells" share employment of a garden motif, of a lover's ghost at the window, and of three-stress lines.*

"More about *Maud.*" Letter. *Home Journal* 20 Oct. 1855: N. pag.
This letter offers a brief and rather weak parody of the garden scene in Maud.

Morse, David. *Romanticism: A Structural Analysis*. Ottowa: Barnese, 1982.
Morse briefly notes a similarity between the narrator of Maud *and Shakespeare's* Hamlet, *based on the influence of fate on the downfall of each.*

"Mr. Tennyson and his *Maud*." *Morning Post* [London] 1 Sept. 1855: 5-6.
In this very negative review, Maud *is cited as evidence that Tennyson ate from the insane root that takes the reason prisoner.* Maud *is treated as an autobiographical poem and a work without luster that taxes the patience of its readers and tears the Laureate's crown to tatters.*

Nencioni, Enrico. "*Maud*." *Domenica Litteraria* 19 Mar. 1882.
See Beetz: entry 1029.

Nishimae, Yoshimi. "A Study of Tennyson's *Maud's* Imagery: With Special
  References to Images of Animals, Jewels, Stones, and Flowers." *Hiroshima Studies in English Language and Literature* 24 (1979): 17-28.
See Beetz: entry 4951.

Oliphant, Margaret. "Modern Light Literature: Poetry." *Blackwood's Magazine* 79
  (Feb. 1856): 125-38. Excerpted in *National Magazine* 8 (June 1856): 432.
Oliphant provides an overall negative review of Maud *that criticizes Tennyson for having assaulted the ears and patience of his reading public with the rantings of a "miserable grumbler." She then links his doing so to the influence and extravagances of the Spasmodic school. However, she does praise Tennyson for having resisted the Spasmodic convention of a poet-hero. Oliphant affirms that a poet's hero ought not to be a poet, for poet-heroes leave readers with a distaste for poetic self-laudation, and, in this sense at least, Tennyson distinguishes himself from the lesser writers known as the Spasmodics.*

---. "Tennyson." *Blackwood's Edinburgh Magazine* 152 (Nov. 1892): 748-66.
Notes how Maud *initially horrified Victorian readers with its unapologetic presentation of the wrongs and injuries of the age, and then describes how, when those wrongs and injuries became too apparent to deny, critics began to praise the mission and merits of the honest monodrama, which she now describes as the most lovely and ethereal of compositions.*

O'Neill, James N. "Anthem for a Doomed Youth: An Interdisciplinary Study of
  Tennyson's *Maud* and the Crimean War." *Tennyson Research Bulletin* 5
  (1990): 166-81.
O'Neill explores the ambiguity surrounding the poem's conclusion and Tennyson's identification, or lack of it, with his jingoistic hero. O'Neill notes the very important, generally overlooked, fact that when England entered the Crimean War in 1854 it was with the support of the British public, and that it was not until 1855 that public opinion turned against it with the resignation of Prime Minister Aberdeen. This resignation occurred three months before Moxon reviewed the proofs of Maud *– most of which was written during a period of enthusiasm for the Crimean war. Thus, the third part of the poem is more an example of bad timing than an anomaly on*

Tennyson's part. He also notes that Tennyson's failed business venture with Matthew Allen, a venture which cost the poet over 3,000 pounds, is at the heart of the poem's denunciation of rampant commercialism.

---. "Scott's *Bride* and Tennyson's *Maud*." *Tennyson Research Bulletin* 7 (1997): 25-31.
O'Neill briefly explores a variety of similarities between Tennyson's Maud *and Sir Walter Scott's* Bride *of Lammermoor, including: the personality and orphaned situation of the heroes–whom he describes as Hamlet-like–the character of their love interests, and the themes of historical change linked to social analysis, madness, and suicide.*

---. "Tennyson's *Maud*: A Reexamination of its Biographical Genesis and Aesthetic Merits." Diss. Bowling Green, 1975.
Highlighting biographical influences and the false values of industrialized Victorian England, O'Neill explores the monodrama as Tennyson's fusion of social analysis and self-analysis.

Otten, Terry Ralph. "Tennyson's *Maud* and *Becket*." *The Deserted Stage: The Search for Dramatic Form in Nineteenth-Century England*. Athens: Ohio UP, 1972. 76-107.
Otten treats Maud *as evidence of Tennyson's desire to create a new dramatic form and also his inability to meld in one form a focus on both plot and character.*

"Our Library Table." *Manchester Weekly Advertiser* 4 Aug. 1855: 6.
See Shannon page 416.

Paige, Lori Ann. *The Unstable Bubble of Inflated Thought: A Study of The Spasmodic Poets*. Diss. U of Mass, 1994. Ann Arbor: UMI. 1994. 9434518.
Paige links the reception of the Spasmodic closet dramas to the reception of Tennyson's Maud.

Parrill, Anna Sue. "Tennyson's *Maud* and Thomas Carlyle." *Innisfree* 7 (1987): 25-32.
Parrill sees in the narrator's move from self interest to duty the influence of the movement from everlasting no to everlasting yea found in Carlyle's works, particularly Sartor Restartus. *She sees the poem as whole as representing Tennyson's shift from his palace of art to Carlylian public leadership. In other words, it is in* Maud *that Tennyson moves from the "dillettantism" of a Byron to the social responsibility of a Goethe.*

Patmore, Coventry. Rev. of *Maud*, by Alfred Tennyson. *Edinburgh Review* 102 (Oct. 1855): 498-519.
Patmore begins by praising In Memoriam *and then faulting* Maud *for lacking precisely the best qualities found in the earlier work. Patmore objects to the narrator being called a hero because he sees him as a moral relativist. As support, he notes that the narrator's moral constitution is such that finding a shell on the seashore is equivalent to killing a man in a duel. Patmore links* Maud *to "Saint Simeon Stylites"*

and suggests that both leave the reader with confusion concerning the boundaries between sanity and madness, between truth and irony, and between vague voluptuousness and distinct concepts.

Pattison, Robert. *Tennyson and Tradition.* Cambridge: Harvard UP, 1979.
Pattison briefly explores Maud *as a graft of the lyric on the dramatic, and a unique dramatic monologue in the depth and accuracy of its portrayal of madness.*

Pearsall, Cornelia Donetta Jean. *Demented Ingenuity: Tennyson, Browning, and the Culture of the Dramatic Monologue.* Diss. Yale, 1991. Ann Arbor: UMI, 1991. 9221349.
Pearsall explores the possibility that critics' inability to see the monodrama as a dramatic fiction engendered the unfortunate impression that Tennyson's poetry as a whole lacks social and political context.

Pease, Alison. "*Maud* and its Discontents." *Criticism* 36.1 (Winter 1994): 101-18.
Pease offers a psychological and New Historicist evaluation of Maud*'s narrator as one who, suffering from a lack of identity, tries to construct one around a variety of signifiers. Thus, the poem challenges the belief that subject and object can be reconciled and that this act results in self-redemption.*

Platizky, Roger. *A Blueprint of His Descent: Madness and Method in Tennyson's Poetry.* Lewisburg: Bucknell UP, 1989.
Continuing the work he began in his dissertation, Platizky provides close textual readings of five of Tennyson's poems: "Lucretius," "Rizpah," "Romney's Remorse," "St Simeon Stylites," and Maud, *in order to explore how the poet's understanding of psychological tensions, and their historical and cultural influences, evolved with and informed his life's work. In his chapter "Maud: Narcissus and the Quest for Familial Reintegration" Platizky describes the speaker's love interest as a projection of his idealized and feared self: an objectification of the ego ideal he reaches out for by attaching himself symbiotically to her, and as the product of a family he can't help but defensively loathes himself for reaching out to. The end result is a vacillation between fragments of the self, each contingent upon the exploitation of the other.*

---. *Madness and Method in Tennyson's Poetry.* Diss. Rutgers, 1985. Ann Arbor: UMI. 1985. 8520395.
This dissertation explores the thematic and cultural significance of madness in five of Tennyson's poems, focusing in particular on how Tennyson reveals an accurate and unsentimental portrait of madness through such features as hallucinations, fixations, dreams and nightmares, erratic mood swings and breaks in chronology.

"Poetry and the Drama." *The Critic* [London] 15 Aug. 1855, 386-87.
Reviews "Maud" and Other Poems *and praises the monodrama for its rapture in expression thought, and imagination but faults its narrative. The reviewer concludes that* Maud *is a collection of lyrics, rather than a unified dramatic work.*

Poetry of the Past Year." *Christian Remembrancer* 31 (Apr. 1856): 268-70.
The reviewer suggests that Tennyson intended to shock his audience with the

monodrama and that he appropriately did so, for poets are, by vocation, teachers. Moreover, they are inclined to lean toward war rather than peace, as great literature derives from conflict. Noting that the poem's eccentricities evolve from the passion for novelty and change common to modern poetry, the reviewer concludes that each purchaser of Maud is to be congratulated for having made so wise a choice.

Rader, Ralph. "The Composition of Tennyson's *Maud*." *Modern Philology* 59
    (1962): 265-69.

Rader reconciles here the superficially conflicting accounts of the monodrama's composition. He begins with Aubrey de Vere's account of having visited Farringford in 1854 as, inspired by Sir John Simeon's suggestion that he build a preceding poem to contextualize the 1837 Tribute *lyric, Tennyson was working on* Maud. *Rader also notes that Simeon's daughter recalled her father's involvement as one in which he saw the* Tribute *lyric at Farringford and was told by the poet that it was intended to belong to a long dramatic poem he had not been able to carry out. In response, Simeon convinced the poet to working on* Maud. *However, W.F. Rawnsley notes that his mother visited Tennyson at Shiplake in 1852 and convinced him to develop a poem around the* Tribute *lyric. Rader reconciles such conflicting accounts by suggesting that Tennyson was working on* Maud *after the 1837 publication of the* Tribute *lyric but put it aside to work on* In Memoriam *and* The Princess, *and that he returned to* Maud *before his intimacy with Simeon and after his account with Rawnsley. Evidence for this account lies in the fact that Tennyson claimed to have written Part III of the monodrama when the cannons were heard booming from battleships in the Solent before the Crimean War, which began on March 24, 1854. This pre-dated Simeon's visit, which we know could not have occurred before June 6 ,1854. Rader's conclusion is that* Maud *was gestating in Tennyson's mind well before Simeon and Rawnsley spoke up for it, and that he may have discussed his plans to extend the* Tribute *lyric with each of them, making their roles those of support rather than invention.*

---.. "Tennyson and Rosa Baring." *Victorian Studies* 5 (1962): 224-60.
Rader describes the influence of Tennyson's relationship with Rosa Baring on the hopeless love interest featured in the monodrama.

---. Tennyson's "*Maud*": *The Biographical Genesis.* Perspectives in Criticism 15.
    Berkeley: U of California P, 1963.

Rader's influential study is built around the premise that in order to fully understand Maud *we must trace Tennyson's biography from 1830 to 1855, focusing in particular on his relationships with Rosa Baring, Sophy Rawnsley, and Emily Sellwood. Rader notes that in 1825 Arthur Eden, his wife, and his stepdaughter Rosa Baring leased Harrington Hall, situated two miles from Sommersby rectory. Tennyson fell passionately in love with Baring, but the affair ended with her engagement to a wealthy suitor named Robert Shafto, a move suggested by Eden and his wife, who were from prominent, wealthy families. Rader thus links Rosa Baring to* Maud *in the influence of love undone by familial greed, and to the passion signified in the red roses of Maud's garden. Rader suggests that in between Tennyson's affair with*

Baring and engagement to Sellwood (1836 and 1838, respectively), the poet may have proposed to, and been rejected by, Sophy Rawnsley, who is associated with the chaste side of Maud, and with the lily she embodies. He also suggests that Tennyson sought in her a substitute for Arthur Hallam. In 1838 Tennyson became engaged to Emily Sellwood but was forced by her parents to break off this engagement in 1840. Rader suggests that this may have been the result of Tennyson's involvement with Allen's financially disastrous investments, which links Emily as well to the theme of love undone by familial greed. When Tennyson was able to marry Sellwood in 1850, according to Rader, Emily became the inspiration for the Maud we know as "Queen lily and rose in one": a fusion of the best of Baring and Rawnsley.

Ray, Gordon. *Tennyson Reads "Maud."* Vancouver: U of British Columbia P, 1968.
Contains mention of Tennyson's linking Maud *and* Hamlet *to Knowles.*

Ricks, Christopher. " 'Peace and War' and *Maud.*" *Notes and Queries* 9 (1962): 230.
Treats the supposed jingoism of Maud *as a fabrication of a diseased mind.*

---. *Tennyson.* New York: Collier, 1972.
This work is particularly important in the fact that it cites a wealth of Tennyson's own comments about Maud. *It thus addresses the narrator's jingoistic sentiments, and Tennyson's own impression of them, at the end of the poem. Critics have misunderstood the ending of* Maud *because they read into it Tennyson's support for the Crimean War, and comments found in this edition will help to clarify that issue.*

Ryals, Clyde de L. "Tennyson's *Maud.*" *Connotation: A Magazine of the Arts* 1 (1963): 12-32.
Ryals praises Maud *as the finest lyric expression of the nineteenth century. He links the monodrama to* Romeo and Juliet *in its portrait of love set in a backdrop of civil strife and family feuding. He sees in the apocalyptic ending of* Maud *an obsession on the part of Tennyson with the idea that the world was on the brink of ruin. In the love story he finds the theme that desire leads to death, and in the work as a whole he finds an affirmation of the value of selflessness.*

Savage, Michael O'Neil. "Prosody and Structure in Tennyson's *Maud.*" Thesis. U of Memphis, 1997.
In this mathematical analysis of the monodrama's structure, Savage examines and redeems Maud *as art for art's sake, a well crafted work regardless of its spirit or mood.*

Schulman, Samuel. "Mourning and Voice in *Maud.*" *SEL* 23 (1983): 633-46.
Schulman sees Maud, *as much as* In Memoriam, *as a poem about death and mourning. He focuses on the poem's various occasions of mourning and private grief, and also how they give way to the public voice of the poet at the work's conclusion. Schulman links* Maud *to* In Memoriam *in that both poems focus on the mind of the mourning survivor. In* Maud, *he analyzes in particular the place of memory in the*

process of mourning, comparing the memorialist side of the hero to the side of him that tries to embrace his love again in the delusion of a phantom. When the hero gives himself up to public good at the end of the poem, Schulman finds in him the poet who let the process of private mourning and memory lead him to a greater social responsibility in his poetry.

Schweik, Robert C. "The 'Peace or War' Passages in Tennyson's *Maud.*" *Notes and Queries* 7 (1960): 457-58.

Schwiek suggests that an 1854 article in Blackwood's, *titled "Peace and War, A Dialogue," may have influenced the ending of* Maud.

Scimone, Anthony James. *The Undercurrent of Failure: A Study of the Construction and Collapse of Personal Myth in Tennyson's Poetry.* Diss. New York U, 1984. Ann Arbor: UMI, 1984. 8421561.

Scimone treats the hero of Maud's *futile attempt to escape into implausible myth.*

Scott, Patrick. "Tennyson's *Maud* I.26 and an Analogue in Tupper." *Tennyson Research Bulletin* 3 (1978): 83-84.

Scott suggests that Maud's *denunciation of Mammonism and civil war, expressed, in particular, in the "Is it peace or war" (I.26) stanza, was influenced by Martin Tupper's 1851 "A Commentary"– which certainly shares its theme and is quite similar in language and tone.*

---. "Tennyson's *Maud* and its American Publishers: A Relationship Considered." *Papers of the Bibliographical Society of America* 83 (1989): 153-167.

Scott treats the commercial aspects of Maud's *initial American publication and reviews and makes the interesting point that while Ticknor and Fields advertised the work as "in press" on June 15th it was not published in America until August 18th. Scott suggests that the delay was facilitated by Fields: at that time the only American publisher with possession of* Maud, *in order to lend copies of the poem to only those reviewers who were inclined to praise, and thus to enhance the commercial value upon publication. Scott's argument is important in that it refutes what is commonly seen as a non-commercially motivated distinction between* Maud's *laudatory American reviews and its negative British reviews.*

Shannon, Edgar. "The Critical Reception of Tennyson's *Maud.*" *PMLA* 68 (1953): 397-417.

This article is extremely important because it brings together in one place a bibliography of the articles and reviews of Maud *published in 1855-1859, including 58 previously unrecorded reviews. Shannon entries are page-referenced in the present bibliography.*

Shatto, Susan. "The Textual Genesis of *Maud.*" *Victorian Authors and Their Works: Revision, Motivations and Modes.* Ed. Judith Kennedy. Athens: Ohio UP, 1991. 11-17.

Shatto describes the monodrama as more autobiographical than In Memoriam *and briefly outlines the history of its composition, beginning with the germ "Oh! That 'twere Possible" in 1854.*

Shaw, David. "Masks of the Unconscious: Bad Faith and Casuistry in the
    Dramatic Monologue." *ELH* 66 (1999) 439-60.
Shaw describes Maud *as an exercise in "double irony," because its speaker is pulled two ways. Its hero lies to himself, but, as the essence of a deception is to mask a truth, he has to possess the truth he is hiding before he can lie. Hence, if he is to conceal from himself the truth that he is already in love with* Maud, *he must know this truth very exactly himself in order to maintain the protective fiction that he hates her. However, the hysteria of his rhetoric betrays him, to the reader and to himself.*

Shepherd, Richard Herne. "The Genesis of Tennyson's *Maud.*" *North American
    Review* 139 (Oct. 1884): 356-61.
Shepherd lists the sections of Maud *that had been previously published and the changes in its subtitle, and he describes various critical reactions to the work in its varied stages. His personal opinion is that* Maud *represents the high point of Tennyson's genius as well as the mid point of his career.*

Shires, Linda M. "*Maud,* Masculinity and Poetic Identity." *Criticism: A Quarterly
    for Literature and the Arts* 29 (1987): 269-90.
Shires describes the monodrama as a poem about gender conflicts in which a rigid gender codes are exposed, deconstructed, and reconstructed. She treats the gender coding of values, of language, of social and economic situation, and of power. While the poem as a whole is typical in its patriarchal constructs, the speaker's masculine voice interrupts itself with feminine lyrics, calling into question the very identities the poem champions.

Slinn, E. Warwick. "Absence and Desire in *Maud.*" *The Discourse of Self in
    Victorian Poetry.* Charlottesville: UP of Virginia, 1991.
Slinn treats the poem's cyclical presentation of absence and desire as mutually generative and destructive.

Smith, Elton. *Tennyson's Epic Drama.* Lanham: UP of America, 1997.
Smith's work is unique in that it treats Maud *as an extension of Tennyson's dramatic history of England: a dramatic cycle that, in itself, is shamefully under-represented in contemporary scholarship. In doing so, it negates the position of those critics who are inclined to see* Maud *as purely lyric, and of those who undervalue the historical relevance of its portrayal of Victorian social concerns because they find offense with its too strident presentation of the Crimean War as an answer to civil war.*

---. "Tendency Versus Correction." *The Two Voices: A Tennyson Study.* Lincoln:
    U of Nebraska P, 1664. 161-183.
Smith treats tension between polar opposites, neither of which may stand individually as truth, as main theme in Tennyson's poetry. He examines Maud *in this framework, focusing, in particular, on the narrator's desire to withdraw into introversion and the forces that lead him to emerge from it and engage the world at large. Neither of the*

two poles can provide the sole truth, or center, of his existence. Thus, the hero seeks through introversion to escape violence and bloodshed, yet he is ironically pulled out of it by a love that leads him, ultimately, to violence, bloodshed, and a final separation with the world around him.

Smith, Goldwin. "The War Passages in *Maud*." *Saturday Review of Politics, Literature, Science, and Art* [London] 3 Nov. 1855: 14-15. Rpt. in *Tennyson: The Critical Heritage.* Ed. John D. Jump. London: Routledge, 1967.

This review is a must for any student of Maud*'s critical reception. Goldwin has penned what this bibliographer sees as a fascinating, well written, reasonable, and unique critique of* Maud*'s jingoistic sentiments. Instead of working himself into self-congratulatory caustic bliss, he quite mildly points out several faults with* Maud*'s presentation of war as a cure for Mammonism. For example, he notes that the British do not go to war; rather, they send hired soldiers to fight for them, and that the poor are no more likely to obtain bread when the taxes that drain the charities must be raised. He also points out, quite accurately in my opinion, that* Maud*, although it is commonly perceived otherwise, is not entirely distinct in the Tennyson canon. Goldwin notes that* Maud *has as an overall theme the seeking of external sensation when an internal effort is the truer and more appropriate cure, a theme found in "Locksley Hall," "The Two Voices," and other poems by Tennyson. In the case of* Maud*, external stimuli is presented as the cure for both a broken heart and the vices of a nation, highlighting the force of circumstances rather that of free will. Goldwin praises the exquisite harmonies and luscious language of* Maud*, even as he rejects the what he describes as its impractical advice concerning internal effort and external stimuli.*

Smith, Ross. "The Sultan: A Note on the Imagery of Tennyson's *Maud*". *Literature in North Queensland* 1 (1972) 24-7.

Smith explores the possibility that Tennyson's uncle Charles is the autobiographical counterpart to Maud*'s brother: the Sultan. In doing so, he briefly explores the monodrama's gem, light, and animal imagery.*

Spatz, Jonas. "Love and Death in Tennyson's *Maud*." *Texas Studies In Literature and Language: A Journal of the Humanities* 16 (1974): 503-10.

Spatz refutes the idea that Maud *is a love poem in the Romantic tradition and a product of Victorian optimism in its conclusion. He appraises it instead as a precursor of twentieth-century poetry. He cites Tennyson's power of psychological analysis as evidence of his modernity. Spatz sees the hero's love for Maud as a neurotic symptom of his violent unconscious desire that evolves into an efficient justification for committing murder. Torn between a desire for power and suicidal urges, the speaker's outrage against civil war is suffused with subconscious fantasies in which he and his race are annihilated. The modernism of the poem thus surfaces in its theme of taking action and avoiding passivity, regardless of the immorality of the actions taken.*

Stalnaker, Bonny Jean. "A Study of Tennyson's *Maud: A Monodrama* as a Precursor of Modern Poetry." Thesis. Auburn U, 1975.
Stalnaker treats the Romantic tones and themes of the monodrama, its Victorian setting and presentation of social problems, and its modern handling of imagery, meter, and psychological realism. Her conclusion is that the monodrama represents a unique, successful artistic integration of past, present, and future modes, and that the negative criticism it has faced is due to its lack of clear categorization.

Stevenson, Catherine Barnes. "Narrative Form and Point of View in *The Princess, Maud,* and *Idylls of the King.*" Diss. New York U, 1973.
Stevenson affirms that critics don't quite know what to make of the work of Tennyson's middle years, as it is not entirely lyric or dogmatic. In response, she explores the monodrama as a work that resists rigid boundaries and necessitates reader response, in particular, through its distancing: its lack of connections, explanations, and justifications, although the monodramatic form itself is the most intimate of forms.

Stirling, James Hutchinson. "Tennyson and his Poetry." *Meliora* 2 (Oct. 1859): 225-48.
See Shannon page 417.

Stokes, Edward. "The Metrics of *Maud.*" *Victorian Poetry* 2 (1964): 97-110.
Stokes provides a thorough and flattering discussion of the work as one of the finest pieces of metrical resourcefulness in English poetry– without passing judgment on whether Tennyson instinctively or deliberately designed it to be such.

Sturman, Christopher. "Arthur Eden and Harrington Hall." *Tennyson Research Bulletin* 5 (1989): 130- 42.
By examining a letter Arthur Hallam wrote to Emily Tennyson, Sturman concludes that Alfred Tennyson first met Rosa Baring in October of 1832.

"The Talk of the Week." *Cambridge Chronicle* 4 Aug. 1855: 4.
See Shannon page 415.

Tennyson, Alfred, and Susan Shatto. *Tennyson's "Maud": A Definitive Edition.* Norman: U of Oklahoma P, 1986.
Shatto provides here a thorough presentation of Maud *'s publication history and its various manuscripts.*

"Tennyson and His *Maud.*" *The Irish Quarterly Review* 19 (Sep. 1855): 453-72.
In a very negative assessment, the reviewer describes the monodrama as a maudlin, disjointed work that ends in a rank nonsensical conclusion. He also links Maud *to Alexander Smith's* A Life Drama *in its style and imagery.*

Tennyson, Hallam. *Alfred Lord Tennyson: A Memoir by His Son.* 2 vols. London, 1897.
This is an important starting place for anyone who wants to explore the sometimes contradictory assertions of Tennyson himself in relation to the monodrama.

"Tennyson's *Maud*." *Bentley's Miscellany* Sept. 1855: 262-65.
Although dedicated primarily to plot summary, this review praises Tennyson for having glorified a just war with earnestness yet mourns the bitterness with which he does so. The reviewer's overall evaluation is that Maud *surpasses "The Princess" but is inferior to* In Memoriam.

"Tennyson's *Maud*." *Dublin University Magazine* Sept. 1855: 332-40.
This review notes that Maud, *which would perhaps have added to the fame of a lesser poet, will not do so for Tennyson. It describes the monodrama as unsatisfying and disjointed on the whole but occasionally full of fire, vigor, tenderness, and passion. The jingoistic sentiments are described as immoderate but in accordance with the fancy of the speaker, and nevertheless the most praiseworthy element of the poem. It suggests that the hero's sentiments, however, are often base, vulgar, and offensive, and that such characteristics cannot be tempered by even the most accomplished use of rhyme and meter. Rather, the beautiful and ornate language with which they are rendered serves only to make them more outrageous.*

"Tennyson's *Maud*." *Home Journal* 15 Sept. 1855: N. pag.
Accuses Tennyson of jingoism yet suggests that the critical bombast directed against the poem in question has been more absurd than anything in it.

"Tennyson's Maud." *National Review* 1 (Oct. 1855): 377-410.
This very negative review describes Maud *as the unwholesome, morbid, and perverted product of exaggeration and selfishness. At its best, it displays fragments of wonderful beauty, but even then the fragments are mixed, in a highly irritating fashion, with the flimsiest of verse.*

"Tennyson's New Poem." *Putnam's Monthly Magazine* (Sept. 1855): 318.
The reviewer praises Maud *as a poem of tragic reality in which the hero's earnestness and the author's skill combine to show the world that England has yet a great poet.*

"Tennyson's New Poems." *Albion* 21 July 1855: 356.
An expectant notice of Maud*'s forthcoming release..*

"Tennyson's New Poems." *MacPhail's Edinburgh Ecclesiastical Journal and
    Literary Review* 20 (Sept. 1855): 120-25.
This reviewer claims to have attempted to shut his or her eyes to any previous critiques of Maud *so as to form an objective opinion of it; however the very vocal nature of the outcry against the monodrama at times made this impossible. Interestingly, this reviewer, who finds* Maud *a beautiful and worthy creation, suggests that had it been published anonymously it would have been met with universal acclaim, and that its release after* In Memoriam, *the poet's finest work, doomed the monodrama to a negative reception. Specifically refuting impressions of the poem as "hazy," this reviewer describes it an unmatched example of the magic art of description, and an example of Tennyson's having crept unaware into the enchanted domain of William Shakespeare.*

Thomas, Anne Cameron. *The Honey of Posion-Flowers: Women and the Feminine in Tennyson's Poetry.* Diss. U of California, Berkeley, 1991. Ann Arbor: UMI, 1991. 9228884.
Thomas treats gender as represented in the rhetoric and themes of Maud, suggesting that in this work, as in his other works, Tennyson both subverted and upheld Victorian gender constraints.

Thompson, John. Rev. of *"Maud" and Other Poems,* by Alfred Tennyson. *Southern Literary Messenger* 21 (1855): 638-39.
Thompson describes the speaker of the monodrama as uncivilized and disagreeable and the work as a whole as a morbid, splenetic, fragmented undertaking unworthy of its author.

Thomson, Alastair. *The Poetry of Tennyson.* New York: Routledge, 1986.
In his chapter on Maud, Thomson provides an excellent and graciously jargon free introduction to the poem. Taking a mid stance between most criticism of the poem, he refutes the notion that the poem is either purely lyric or entirely dramatic, offering instead of rigid categorization a clear, general introduction to the work's movement, its construction, and its imagery.

Trilling, Lionel, and Bloom, Harold, eds. "Victorian Prose and Poetry." *The Oxford Anthology of English Literature.* 5th ed. Oxford: Oxford UP, 1973.
On page 466, the editors refer to the narrator of Maud as a parody of Tennyson himself and a hero who is absurdly jingoistic at the end of the poem.

Truss, Tom J., Jr. "Tennysonian Aspects of *Maud.*" *University of Mississippi Studies in English* 1 (1960): 105-17.
See Beetz: entry 3719.

Tucker, Herbert. "Maud and the Doom of Culture." *Critical Essays on Alfred Lord Tennyson.* Ed Herbert Tucker. New York: G. K. Hall, 1993. 174-94.
Tucker describes the monodrama as Tennyson's most complete fusion of the public and private modes. He notes that by using the monodramatic form Tennyson was able to circumvent his weakness at imagining other minds, and focus on depicting moods, yet, because he renders the hero's emotional responses to situations drawn from contemporary life, the work has a social context even as it denies the social interaction Tennyson the dramatist appears to have craved. Tucker sees the hero's inability to objectively find causes and effects behind social and personal ills as leading to a baffled passion that dismantles social responsibility, and leads to what Tucker describes as Tennyson's familiar vision of doom. Tucker interesting ties the speaker's love interest to the Victorians desire to subvert the increasingly material effects of love, linking eroticism to power and language, although I can't help but disagree with his suggestion that Tennyson's demand for social acceptance of Maud proves that he found it impossible to endorse the work wholeheartedly.

Turner, Paul. *Tennyson.* London: Routledge, 1996.
Turner provides a fairly comprehensive if not in depth introduction to Maud's literary

influences. In his chapter on Maud, Turner suggests that the monodrama may have been influenced by poems Tennyson read in the Tribute: *the work in which the "O That 'Twere Possible" section had originally been published, and a variety of other possible literary influences, including a linking of* Maud's *overall plot to that of Scott's* The Bride of Lammermoor, *its theme of civil war to* Hamlet, *of love to* Romeo and Juliet, *of madness to the work of the Spasmodic poets, and of the denunciation of peace to Carlyle's* Past and Present. *Turner also describes the fashion in which the monodrama was composed backwards, the influence of Tennyson's direct experience with Matthew Allen, and the Rosa Baring connection to* Maud. *Particularly useful and rare is his connection between the landscape of the Isle of Wight and the geological references in* Maud.

Vanden Bossche, Chris R. "Realism Versus Romance: The War of Cultural Codes in Tennyson's *Maud." Victorian Poetry* 24 (1986): 69-82.
Bossche notes some of the incongruities in Tennyson's own accounts of the monodrama and ties them to the tension between realism and romanticism found in the poem itself: a tension between reading realistically what is essentially a romance plot featuring courtship, chivalry, and love.

Van Dyke, Henry. *"The Princess" and "Maud." The Poetry of Tennyson: A Book of Essays in Vital Criticism.* New York: Scribner's, 1900.
Van Dyke notes that his early underrating and misunderstanding of Maud *changed into appreciation and acclaim after he heard Tennyson read the monodrama aloud. He then paraphrases many of Tennyson's own comments on the poem, including: that the work is a drama in lyrics, that each lyric traces the evolution of his madness under the influence of love, and that the poem's faults are those of the hero's madness, not of the work itself. While refuting some of these assertions, Van Dyke praises the poem for its imagery, mellifluous language, and presentation of intense, ennobling love.*

Victor, O.J. Rev. of *Maud*, by Alfred Tennyson. *Lady's Repository* 18 (July 1858): 420-23.
Victor accuses Tennyson of morbidity and jingoism and describes Maud *as unworthy of its creator's genius.*

Waddington, Patrick. *Tennyson and Russia.* Tennyson Society Monographs 11. Lincoln: Tennyson Society, 1987.
Waddington describes the influence of Russian history, and the acquaintance of Russian writers, on Tennyson's poetry.

Walters, J. Cuming. *Tennyson: Poet, Philosopher, Idealist: Studies of the Life, Work, and Teaching of the Poet Laureate.* New York: Haskell, 1971.
In his brief chapter on Maud, *Walters praises the poem's martial vigor, its implied lesson, its pathos, and its musical flights.*

Walton, James. "Tennyson's Patrimony: From *The Outcast* to *Maud." Texas Studies in Literature and language: A Journal of the Humanities* 11 (1969): 733-59.

Walton treats the narrator of Maud as the victim of a childhood oedipal complex.

Weiner, S. Ronald. "The Chord of Self: Tennyson's *Maud*." *Literature and Psychology* 16 (1966): 175-83.
Weiner explores the speaker's ambivalence toward love as the product of his father's death, a death that creates a psychological tension between his role as a lover and his role as a dutiful son. Weiner also describes what he sees as the speaker's oedipal complex and its relationship to his sub-conscious desire to embrace self-destruction. Weiner, like Basler, sees Maud as an example of Tennyson's having anticipated Freud in his recognition of the complex phases of self, his focus on the unconscious, and his general theme of psychic phenomena.

White, Clyde Patrick. "Tennyson's *Maud* as a Spasmodic Poem." Thesis. U of Virginia, 1962.
White links Maud to the Spasmodic closet dramas in characterization, form, and style

Wordsworth, Jonathan. "Double Meanings III. 'What is it that has Been Done?':The Central Problem of *Maud*." *Essays in Criticism: A Quarterly Journal of Literary Criticism* 24 (1974): 356-62.
Wordsworth treats the narrator's attitudes and actions as engendered by a childhood Oedipal trauma through which love for his mother evolved into a hatred for his father and various father surrogates.

W. "New Poetry, English and American." *Evening Transcript* [Boston] 19 Dec. 1855: N. pag.
W. describes Maud as one of his favorite works: a work of truth and the grandest passions humanity is capable of, a work full of noble thoughts and brilliant pictures, and a work misunderstood by a careless uneducated populace.

Wolfe, Humbert. *Tennyson.* Poets on Poets 3. London: Faber and Faber, 1930.
Wolfe praises Maud as the first modernist poem and a pre-curser to Eliot's "The Wasteland."

Y. "Value of Half an Hour." Letter. *Home Journal* 27 Oct. 1855: N. pag.
Y. praises Maud as a work of exquisite loveliness and sentiment.

Notes

Chapters One Through Four

1. See Buckley's *The Victorian Temper*, 44-45; Collins' "Tennyson and the Spasmodics, 25; and Paige's "The Unstable Bubble of Inflated Thought"(entry on page 113).

2. For a full analysis of *Isabella*, see Hilton, pages 35 though 38.

3. An unfortunate consequence of the popularity of Goethe's *The Sorrows of Young Werther* was the symbolic tribute to Werther, popular among young men of Europe, which involved dressing up in his deathbed costume, a yellow waistcoat and blue jacket, and taking one's own life. Many of the young painters associated with the Romantic movement painted subjects, including themselves, in the Werther "costume." The outfit itself thus became an important symbol of the Romantic obsession with the transience of life and beauty that must die. See J.M.W. Turner, *Self-Portrait* (1799), Tate Gallery, London.

4. Dante Gabriel Rossetti's 1855 sketch, "Tennyson Reading *Maud,*" the Birmingham Museum and Art Gallery.

5. For an excellent introduction to German Naturphilosophie and the symbolic presentation of caves and cave mining– particularly potent symbols for Romantics such as E.T.A. Hoffmann, J.M.W. Turner, and Mary Shelley– see Nicholas Rupke's "Caves, Fossils, and the History of the Earth," *Romanticism and the Sciences*, eds. Andrew Cunningham and Nicolas Jardine (Cambridge: Cambridge UP, 1990. 241-259).

6. Johann Rosenmuiller was one of the German Naturphilosophers who championed the Romantic myth of caves as corridors into the secret workshops of Mother Nature. He was particularly interested in extinction and degeneration. See Rupke 241-259.

7. Charles Lyell's highly influential three volume *Principles of Geology* (1830-1833) proposes that the earth is a byproduct of an endless march of natural forces, such as wind and water erosion, that will eventually engender the extinction of all living species.

8. Compare lines 3-5 of "Ulysses": "I mete and dole / Unequal laws unto a savage race / That hoard, and sleep, and feed, and know not me" to *Hamlet*'s 4.4. 33-50: "What is a man if his chief good and market of his time / Be but to sleep and feed? A beast, no more."

9. It was not uncommon for the Victorians to associate biological degeneration with the criminal sensibility. Cesare Lombroso referred to criminals as "atavisms," the progeny of a less evolved strain of human being. See Gina Lombroso Ferrero's *Criminal Man According to the Classification of Cesare Lombroso* (New York, 1911).

10. Neptunism is based on the theory that the Earth was covered by water until chemical precipitation led crystalline rocks to form and the water to recede. As Neptunism allows for both degeneration and progress, many of the Romantics saw it a metaphor for the striving of the individual. In response, many Romantic scientists attempted to map our evolution from amphibian to human form. The narrator may be acknowledging this view when he describes the eft as an ancestral figure. See Rupke 241-259.

11. A.G. Werner was a famous Neptunist. See Rupke 241-259.

References

Excludes Works Listed in Chapter Four

Aries, Philippe. *Images of Man and Death*. Trans. Janet Lloyd. Cambridge: Harvard UP, 1985.

Aytoun, William Edmondstoune. *Firmilian: A Spasmodic Tragedy,* by T. Percy Jones. New York, 1854.

---. Rev. of *Firmilian*, by T. Percy Jones. *Blackwood's Magazine* 75 (1854): 533-51.

Bailey, Philip James. *Festus: A Poem*. Boston, 1860.

Black, Greta. "Bailey's Debt to Goethe's *Faust*." *Modern Language Review* 28 (1933):166-75.

Cruse, Amy. *The Victorians and Their Reading*. Boston: Houghton, 1935.

Dobell, Sydney Thompson. *Balder. Part the First.* London, 1854.

---. *The Life and Letters of Sidney Dobell*. 2 vols. London, 1878.

Eliot, T.S.. "Interpretation of the major Poems: *In Memoriam*." *Tennyson's Poetry*. Ed. Robert W. Hill. New York: Norton, 1971. 613-20.

Rev. of *Festus,* by Philip Bailey. *Blackwood's Magazine* 67 (April 1850): 415-30.

Fitzgerald, F. Scott. *The Great Gatsby*. Hertfordshire: Wordsworth, 1993.

Gilbert, Sandra and Susan Gubar. *The Madwoman in the Attic: The Woman Writer and the Nineteenth-Century Literary Imagination*. New Haven: Yale UP, 1979.

Gilfillan, George. "A New Poet in Glasgow." *Critic: London Literary Journal* (Dec. 1851): 567.

Girouard, Mark. *The Return to Camelot: Chivalry and the English Gentleman.* New Haven: Yale UP, 1981.

Gosse, Edmund William. *Portraits and Sketches*. London, 1912.

Gould, Stephen Jay, "Red in Tooth and Claw." *Natural History* 101.1 (1992): 14-23.

Hagen, June Steffensen. "Tennyson Praises the Spasmodics: A Second Conversation With the Scottish Mr. Mitchell." *Tennyson Research Bulletin* 2 (1974): 74-75.

Harris, Jack. "I have Never Seen a Naked Lady of Shalott." *The Journal of Pre-Raphaelite Studies* 5 (1984): 76-87.

Hill, Robert W. Introduction. *Maud*, by Alfred Tennyson. *Tennyson's Poetry*. Ed. Robert W. Hill. New York: Norton, 1971. 214.

Hilton, Timothy. *The Pre-Raphaelites*. New York: Thames, 1989.

Hunt, William Holman. *Isabella and the Pot of Basil*.1868. Tyne and Wear Museum.

Lambourne, Lionel. *The Aesthetic Movement*. London: Phaidon, 1996.

Leng, Andrew. "*Mariana*: Literary Painting, the Pre-Raphaelite Gothic, and the Iconology of the Marian Artist." *The Journal of Pre-Raphaelite and Aesthetic Studies* 1(1988): 63-74.

Lourie, Margaret. "Below the Thunders of the Upper Deep: Tennyson as Romantic Revisionist." *Studies in Romanticism*. 18 (1979): 3-27.

"Matthew: 26." *New International Bible*. Bible Gateway. Online. Internet. 12 Feb. 2001.

Maudsley, Henry, M.D. *Body and Will: Being an Essay Concerning Will in its Metaphysical, Physiological, and Pathological Aspects*. New York, 1884.

Millais, John Everett. *Lorenzo and Isabella*. 1849. Walker Art Gallery, Liverpool.

---. *Mariana*. 1851. Makins private collection.

Morse, David. *Romanticism: a Structural Analysis*. Ottowa: Barnes, 1982.

Poulson, Christine. "Death and the Maiden: The Lady of Shalott and the Pre-Raphaelites." *Re-Framing the Pre-Raphaelites: Historical and Theoretical Essays*. Ed. Ellen Harding. Brookfield: Scolar, 1996.

Rossetti, Christina. "Goblin Market." *The Norton Anthology of English Literature*. 7th ed. Vol. 2B: The Victorian Age. Ed. M.H. Abrams. New York: Norton, 2000. 1589-1601.

Rossetti, Dante Gabriel. *Beata Beatrix*. 1863. The Tate Gallery, London.

---. "The Blessed Damozel." *The Norton Anthology of English Literature*. 7th ed. Vol. 2B: The Victorian Age. Ed. M.H. Abrams. New York: Norton, 2000. 1574-77.

Rossetti, Michael, and William Fredeman. *The P.R.B. Journal: William Michael Rossetti's Diary of the Pre-Raphaelite Brotherhood 1849-53*. Oxford: Clarendon, 1975.

Shakespeare, William, and Susanne Wofford. *Hamlet*. Case Studies in Contemporary Criticism 6. Boston: Bedford, 1994.

Smith, Alexander. *A Life Drama and Other Poems*. Boston, 1870.

---. *Dreamthorpe*. London, 1863.

---. "Sydney Dobell." *Argosy* 2 (1866): 313-28.

"The Spasmodic School." *North British Review* 45 (Scpt. 1866): 83-84.

Stein, Richard. "The Pre-Raphaelite Tennyson." *Victorian Studies* 24 (1981): 279-301.

Tennyson, Alfred Lord. "The Lady of Shalott." *Tennyson's Poetry*. Ed. Robert W. Hill. New York: Norton, 1971. 13-16.

---. "Mariana." *Tennyson's Poetry*. Ed. Robert W. Hill. New York: Norton, 1971. 6-7.

---. "Maud: A Monodrama." *Tennyson's Poetry*. Ed. Robert W. Hill. New York: Norton, 1971. 214-47.

---. "Tithonus." *Tennyson's Poetry*. Ed. Robert W. Hill. New York: Norton, 1971. 71-72.

---. "Ulysses." *Tennyson's Poetry*. Ed. Robert W. Hill. New York: Norton, 1971. 52-53.

Waterhouse, John. *The Lady of Shalott*. Tate Gallery, London.